Vatican Confidential

Also by Cardinal Gerhard Müller
from Sophia Institute Press:

Benedict and Francis
Roman Encounter

Vatican Confidential
A Candid Conversation
with Cardinal Gerhard Müller

Cardinal Gerhard Müller
with Franca Giansoldati

Translated by Nicholas Reitzug

SOPHIA INSTITUTE PRESS
Manchester, New Hampshire

Sophia Institute Press
Box 5284, Manchester, NH 03108
1-800-888-9344
www.SophiaInstitute.com

Sophia Institute Press is a registered trademark of Sophia Institute.

paperback ISBN 979-8-88911-104-7

ebook ISBN 979-8-88911-105-4

Library of Congress Control Number: 2023943751

First printing

Contents

Preface

by Franca Giansoldati

There is a fragment of the Gospel that, more than any other, has worked a magnetic attraction on Gerhard Müller: a sort of call that he heard in the background at every step of his life:

> You shall love the Lord your God with all your heart, and with all your soul, and with all your mind.... You shall love your neighbor as yourself. On these two commandments depend all the law and the prophets. (Matt. 22:37–40)

During his studies in the seminary as a youth, that passage from Matthew emerged imperiously, striking him with intensity: "For me it was a pressing appeal. Naturally, giving preference to one passage of the Gospel over another is a complicated matter for a theologian, but those words effectively changed me." The cardinal, one of the most authoritative theology scholars, curator of the monumental sixteen-volume work on Joseph Ratzinger, knows that the Word contained in the Gospels is systemic and, in its entirety, clearly indicates the road to travel.

Entering his house, the same apartment where Joseph Ratzinger lived for twenty years, in an austere building just beyond the confines of the Vatican, gives the impression of entering a library. The walls lined with volumes from floor to ceiling dampen the noise. The shelves are organized by subject: philosophy, dogmatics, biblical sciences, moral theology; but there is also space for the great books, with a certain predilection for Dostoyevsky. "I've never seen anyone sound the depths of the human soul like him."

Tens of thousands of books in nine languages. "Better to read and study the original texts and not in translation; otherwise, something is always lost along the way, and the texts are impoverished of important nuances," the cardinal explained to me as he showed me around. Our interviews took place in his study over a period of time, and from them, this book has come to life. Müller felt the need to pause and reflect on the weakening of Catholic doctrine and to find an explanation for the numerous theological interpretations that are fermenting in various parts of the world. As he tells in different passages of this book, the cardinal, once prefect of the Congregation for the Doctrine of the Faith, has always placed at the heart of his work the safeguarding and conservation of the Faith, seeking to protect it from insidious interpretations that have emerged. "My assessment has always been constructive. If I saw something that needed highlighting, I knew it was my task to do so. How could I have kept silent? I never acted unfaithfully toward Pope Francis, and God is my witness. The mass media labeled me as a cardinal contrary to the current pontificate because of my precision, but this is not true. It is a falsehood." The book set out with these premises, as if to remove all prejudices from the field. Then we agreed on the rules to follow for fulfilling it. In essence, they can be condensed in a few points.

It was fundamental for me to be able to ask the cardinal any question and obtain from him answers free of diplomatic filters. The cardinal accepted after a few minutes of silence, asking me to be precise in reporting his thought, his analyses, and every explicative passage to be considered opportune.

While he spoke the first day, a volume of Hannah Arendt that dealt with the origins of totalitarianism was open on a little table next to me. Seeing that I was interested in it, Müller anticipated me: "It's not the only volume I'm reading at the moment. In general, I read a number of works contemporaneously. Where do I find the time? I hardly ever watch TV, and when I travel, I pass the time with books."

Müller was the prefect of the Congregation for the Doctrine of the Faith until 2016, and before that, he was the archbishop of Regensburg, where he also taught theology at the university, publishing some forty works, translated into numerous languages. Benedict XVI had the idea of bringing him to Rome and proposed that he take his place at the Holy Office after he was elected pope in 2005, after the death of John Paul II. In this key role, Müller saw on his desk the most pressing dossiers, some even repellent, seeking always to identify the best path to guard the "right doctrine." That role was maintained until 2016, when Pope Francis dismissed him without warning, linking his decision to the fact that Müller had exceeded the five-year limit of service in the Curia and needed to leave space for others. This is an administrative rule of recent coinage that had hitherto never been applied with consistency. Some heads of dicasteries, in fact, have remained in their roles for many more years, having this rule waived for them without a precise motivation being given. For a German like Müller, raised on bread and codes, disregarding the rules in force is like injecting a virus into a system to create confusion — in the end, an injustice, the equivalent of an exhibition of incomprehensible power. Müller recalls the initial shock because there were no motives and because, even later, he was never given any explanation. It was simply an "arbitrary choice."

Freed from the weight of the congregation, Müller began to travel the world giving conferences, called by bishops, cardinals, communities, foundations, universities, dioceses, and lay research centers. Thanks to this articulated activity, he has come to realize that the

Church is weakening — as if it were a blanket going threadbare, something in retreat, at times even tired. What alarms Müller is the general tendency to disperse the patrimony of faith due to widespread doctrinal confusion. In simple words, he sees advancing in the Church, at every level, a current of thought inclined to consider the figure of Jesus Christ at the level of a brother, a friend, a good person, an example of moral living, but no longer as the one Mediator between God and men, the Son become Savior of the world, the Word made flesh. The German theologian distinguishes the shape of what once characterized the ancient heresies — for example, Pelagianism. This means observing the advance of a Church without the Cross that is being transformed, step by step, into a great NGO with mainly humanitarian features.

In the conversations that followed, the cardinal went into depth analyzing world events, developing his analysis, and focusing on the future challenges for Christianity. He imagined how faith might respond — in ten, twenty, or thirty years — to man's existential questions, when artificial intelligence will have entered into daily life, and a different relationship will be established between the individual and machines, developing in man new philosophical and religious queries. Müller did not avoid any questions. Regarding the problems raised by the emeritus pontiff Joseph Ratzinger — presenting his resignation in 2013 — he asked if and how that historic event might affect the papacy today and pontificates to come, delving into the particulars of many episodes of Vatican incidents generally destined to remain behind the scenes. The historical and theological role of Rome as the center of Christianity was examined, and the cardinal asserts in various passages, "The Church is in Jesus Christ the universal sacrament of salvation and not an association created by man, whose structure can be modified by her members at will."

Müller remains convinced that by the next pontificate, Church leaders will have to speak to the world with fewer pressures and less conditioning with respect to those pressures imposed under the weight of mass media or the influence of the politically correct. The search for compromise in order to placate the world is the reason for the disintegration of doctrine. The Church will be saved only if she will have the strength to go against the grain and to "shout from the rooftops" the Faith according to the teaching of gospel memory. "Not always easy," the cardinal admits. In a globalized world in which communication is in real time, Müller considers transparency and integrity indispensable compasses; otherwise, our image of the Church turns opaque, eroding the trust of the faithful.

His vision is based on the Second Vatican Council. He never takes on critical reflections for judging negatively the figure of Francis. At times, he analyzes critical points with great candor but always with loyalty and respect. According to his way of seeing things as a German theologian, reading without filters remains his hermeneutical tool for cooperating in the good of the Church. He reminds us that, in the past, there were authoritative theologians in the Vatican Curia — for example, Robert Bellarmine — who got into trouble for guarding the Faith and for having limited theological errors that would have taken the Church for a ride. Not that Müller wants to compare himself to Bellarmine. When I pointed this out to him, he started laughing. That historical example was meant to help us understand how a certain conformism to the figure of the pontiff can be considered physiological and, now as then, has impeded the Curia from expressing themselves openly without fear or conditioning.

The great theological discussions in these years, beginning with the Synod on the Family, include other more delicate questions, from abortion to end-of-life care. Rules remain the pillars for this former professor of dogmatics. "When the norms fall apart, chaos enters into any system." Müller even jokes about it: "Maybe it's my being German, but without a bit of discipline everything becomes unmanageable." He does not hide his concern for Germany and the approaching schism, or for the destiny of Europe or the political situation in China. On the international level, he deals with the phases of the war in Ukraine with grief, and inevitable memories of his childhood come to mind: the Second World War had just ended with the defeat of an entire people, his German people, bewitched by devastating and malicious Nazi ideology. The temptation to manipulate the masses is a risk he sees on the horizon today as well.

As a former professor and a man of culture, he often draws on a historical and biblical repertory to find apt examples. "At this moment, I see the Church on the edge of a precipice": just a few words to make us understand the need to return to the essential, to the spirit of the origins, to the patrimony of the Faith that the Church has guarded over the centuries while renewing her presence in the world. It might be a way to set off anew — like the yeast of biblical memory.

In recent years, internal lacerations produced by a series of events have led several cardinals openly to denounce supposed theological deviations, such as the ease in unbinding Catholic marriages introduced by the apostolic exhortation *Amoris Laetitia*, the concluding document of the Synod on the Family. Certain risks to the integrity of doctrine could be hiding within the lines of that text. For Müller, this is a break with the past and with the spirit of the gospel, in which the inviolability of sacramental marriage is emphasized. The cardinals who publicly raised this issue wrote the pontiff a letter in which were collected their theological doubts, but they were never given an audience or even a response. The pope preferred to let the matter slide. Müller considers that moment a watershed, seeing how it left an open wound unhealed and dug a trench between two visions. On one side were the hardliners, attentive to form, norms, and doctrinal precision; on the other, the openers, oriented toward creative paths that might open the Church to the needs of those with failed marital experiences and families reconstructed in second "marriages."

As a collateral effect of the presence of two pontiffs in the Vatican, two main parties have taken shape in these years — on one side, those more inspired by Ratzinger and, on the other, those inspired by Francis — in a dualism previously unknown. The polarization has nourished over time a request for radical reforms (female priesthood, blessings for gay couples, direct election of bishops, the abolition of priestly celibacy), while, on the opposite side, there has been a hardening of perspective. In fact, for years now, a certain theological conformism has taken over that pretends to defend Pope Francis from the "party" of the conservatives, explaining that the pope has touched not doctrine but only pastoral practice. The Church historian Alberto Melloni has poignantly observed, in this regard, that acting thus, one offends, in a single blow, doctrine ("it is not a monolith but a hierarchy of truths"),[1] pastoral practice (it is an adjective describing Jesus' way of being and not the marketing of the sacred for dupes), and the Successor of Peter (who is a teacher of faith and not an armed guard placed in front of a bank vault).

Müller is a guardian, and his vision seems to be a compass for understanding the bases on which the next conclave will move and which theological themes the electors will have to engage when choosing a successor to Francis. No one can hazard a guess; it is all too premature. However, the state of laceration in the Church imposes a far-reaching examination. For the moment, the College of Cardinals from which the next pontiff will be chosen is punctually renewed as the electors reach the threshold for voting of eighty years. Their number is maintained above the 120 members according to the arrangement of Pope Paul

[1]   See T. Alex Giltner, "A Cardinal Misunderstanding of the Hierarchy of Truths," *Catholic World Report*, February 8, 2023, https://www.catholicworldreport.com/2023/02/08/a-cardinal-misunderstanding-of-the-hierarchy-of-truths/.

VI. Pope Francis has rendered the College of Cardinals more international in these years, the reflection of a global Church going out to the peripheries by choosing, above all, figures from these peripheries of the world. They are certainly men gifted with human depth, but they are little known on the international level, with rare exceptions. The same members do not know each other well, and yet the future of the Church will depend on them. With this book, Müller provides a simple, analytical, exhaustive framework on the state of matters: a unprecedented hermeneutical tool for helping us to understand better what is at stake. And above all, it provides lenses that offer an analysis "in good faith," as the title of the book suggests, with sincerity and the will to adhere to Catholic orthodoxy until the very end.

A Guardian

Much has been written about you as a theologian, and your works are translated around the world, but little is known about your life. Who is Cardinal Gerhard Ludwig Müller?

I am one of the eight billion people on the planet. We are creatures of God, desired and called to participate in eternal life. We are sinners in need of forgiveness — all of us. In the brief time we reside on this earth, we must exercise our talents to the best of our abilities and take responsibility for others, for society, and for the Church. All of this can be concentrated in one question: What is the meaning of life? The decidedly nihilistic vision of the world tells us that everything is chance, including our existence. But are we not, rather, people desired by God with a definitive eternal destiny of participation in the divine life? Every day, we ought to reflect upon this question. I do so, and I find it a good practice because it is one of the great challenges of our age: the hermeneutics of being, of how one comprehends and interprets not only oneself but also individual existence in relation to the fundamental orientation of loving God and one's neighbor. This is an intellectual and spiritual reference point, a very concrete amalgamation that leads us by the hand along the paths of this planet and in this universe, which we know is immense. We must not be afraid, for we are children of God. With this same awareness, we know that all are equal in relationship to the Creator, and this, obviously, offers each of us the possibility to accept the legitimate differences that exist, receiving each being as a member of the same human family.

Let's come back down to earth: Where were you born? Can you tell me about your origins in Germany, about your father and mother, your studies, your decision to become a priest, your experience as an academic, and the theological path that led you to Peru?

I certainly did not descend from the heavens [*laughs heartily*]. I was born near Mainz, in Germany, of two loving, very hardworking parents — simple people, down to earth, and full of faith. My existence is certainly the result of many preceding generations, my ancestors, although I am not the result of chance. I am the last of four children, two girls and two boys. Unfortunately, none of them are still living, though by good fortune, I have many nieces and nephews and grandnieces and grandnephews. I consider mine to be a good family, a family like so many who grapple with daily problems, fatigue, and sacrifice. My mother cared for us children, for our growth. My parents raised us with love and a certain amount of discipline, although not perhaps excessively German, as one might imagine (to use a cliché that often recurs when speaking of us Germans).

I come from the Rhine region, where the ancient roots of the Roman Empire are deeply felt: not a very Prussian influence, surely less conditioned by the rigid stamp of Bismarck than one might normally think. The stereotypical image of Germans and of Germany strains to take into account the great cultural differences that are still present in the country. It was never a homogenous country. This can be translated, to synthesize, into a mentality that is more or less prone to a certain rigorous discipline, almost military, typical of some regions in Germany, although it is not the distinctive trait of the area I come from and in which I was raised. In Mainz, we even jest about this diversity and laugh over it, saying that the Prussian state born in Brandenburg is not a state with an army but, rather, an army with a state. My state was influenced heavily by Roman culture and by its proximity to France. Catholics are more numerous than in other areas where the Lutheran presence predominates. Even though I have lived in Rome for years, I have maintained strong ties with my homeland.

I was born in a town called Finthen, from the Roman name Ad Fontes. The name refers to springs from which a long aqueduct carried water to Mainz, about five miles away, in Roman times. Today, only an archaeological site remains of that structure. It came to light on the last day of the year 1947, St. Sylvester's Day. The war had ended not long before. It was an occupied zone, first by the French and then by the Americans, and I would say that this aspect, too, had a certain relevance if you compare it with the zones that were occupied by the Russians in the eastern areas of Germany. In hindsight, I can say I was fortunate to have grown up under the spirit of Konrad Adenauer. As a youth, I saw how the war had left enormous problems in the land — wounds and laceration. The memory of what had happened was oppressive; it marked the lives of families. Every hearth mourned the loss of the fallen and relatives missing or maimed. There was desperation. In my town, three thousand inhabitants in all, more than three hundred had died — 10 percent — and, of course, they were all young men. In my home, too, we often spoke of those who were no more. A cousin of my father had been killed at Montecasino, and another uncle, only twenty years old, had fallen at Stalingrad. These men were used as cannon fodder by Hitler to fight and fill out the ranks of the Wehrmacht.

My family always opposed the Third Reich. My mother vehemently detested Adolf Hitler and considered him a dangerous criminal. My father attributed the collective tragedy to the Führer. My parents, practicing Catholics, considered Nazism a pseudo-religion from which to keep one's distance because it was contrary to the teachings of Christianity and because it denied God. My mother recounted that when, as a youth, she heard Hitler's speeches on the radio, she ran away frightened by the unbearable, threatening tone. Those who lived under the Third Reich, refusing it or opposing it, lived in constant fear. The atmosphere was intolerable, and the anguish of those opposed to Nazism was a common denominator. Those who expressed contrary ideas were severely punished and at times were sent to prison and tortured. The bishop of Mainz was one of the few bishops who, in 1933, prohibited Catholics in his region from voting for and belonging to the Nazi Party. He was a courageous man; his name was Ludwig Maria Hugo, and he set a great example for me. Naturally, he was not the only German bishop to stand in opposition after Pius XI's 1937 encyclical *Mit Brennender Sorge*, which openly condemned Nazism, due to its anthropology in complete contrast to Christianity and its negation of man and even of God.

I imagine that, for any German, the historical memory of the war is still a heavy burden to bear. Besides courageous figures such as the bishop of Mainz and the archbishop of Münster, others showed acquiescence, supporting National Socialism. It was not a pretty page of history for the Church.

Unfortunately, after 1933, with National Socialism's rise to power, the Catholic Church as an institution was forced to recognize Adolf Hitler as democratically elected and therefore had to consider his authority legitimate. A certain pragmatism prevailed, and the Church sought a path of coexistence. I think she did so in an attempt to limit the evil intrinsic to that ill-fated ideology. Obviously, I do not wish to justify this terrible and even incomprehensible transition but only to contextualize it. It's similar to what is happening today in China, where there is a system led by one party, decidedly illiberal, but with which the Vatican is seeking a difficult path of compromise on behalf of the Chinese Church.

Returning to the topic of Germany, and without making comparisons that might derail us, when Pius XI's encyclical *Mit Brennender Sorge* was read from the pulpit in German churches, it was clear to the faithful that there could be no ideological affinity of any sort between Nazism and the Christian vision, that it was unacceptable to theorize about the supremacy of the Aryan race over other races, in a diabolical hierarchy that placed the Jews at the bottom; for us Christians, the people of Israel are the Chosen People, theologically speaking. The news reported harsh reactions. The response to that Sunday reading, in fact, was brutal, and the Nazis began to persecute whoever opposed them, those who distributed materials or printed simple pamphlets. They punished many priests, catechists, and laypeople. In the Diocese of Mainz, nearly half the priests were reprimanded by the Nazis. Some were placed in concentration camps, others killed outright, before the eyes of their parishioners; others had to pay high fines for having hindered the regime. Everyone was under surveillance, and, in fact, it was prohibited to preach or speak against Hitler. And *Mit Brennender Sorge* was banned.

As a German, how do you perceive the sense of collective guilt for what happened in Germany? I'm referring to the extermination camps, the Shoah, the deaths of six million people.

We Christians are theologically opposed to assigning collective guilt. Every one of us is accountable for what he has done and for what he does. The people, to some extent, can be considered culpable in this framework, and it is never easy to live with this heavy burden on one's shoulders, even when it is a matter of things done by others that happened decades ago. The reference is to those who, at that time, were in command of the state and its institutions. They were the ones who acted on behalf of the Germans. They dragged them into it and galvanized them, progressively manipulating them. It was a diabolical project. Naturally, those who live outside Germany will struggle to apply precise distinctions, for example, between the SS and the Wehrmacht, between the elite troops (downright fanatics) and the young men forced to go and fight. For the European populations invaded and occupied with so much violence (the Poles come to mind first, though not only them), the German soldiers were always indistinct: which military formation they belonged to, whether the Wehrmacht or the SS, mattered to no one. As a German, I think one has to make a clear separation between those who were truly leading the German state and those who were not.

If we go back and watch the tapes of that era, it is difficult to understand this type of explanation. There were millions of people in the streets, and all of them sang Hitler's praises in unison. A collective madness, almost demonic. Primo Levi wrote about his encounters in Auschwitz, among the ranks of the wardens, with men just like him, neither crazy nor sadistic. Common men.

Nothing can be compared to the Shoah. It was evil raised to the level of a system — unique as such, and nothing can diminish it. The roots, however, of this ferocious and diabolical dynamic that brought the masses into complicity can be found elsewhere, too, and in other historical periods. Take, for instance, the Terror during the French Revolution: it's enough to read the accounts of that time, quite detailed in their descriptions of the ferocity on the streets of France. Perhaps one should always analyze the precise moment in which a people loses its moral principles and falls into the web of propaganda and hate, transforming an entire context into uncontrolled, dangerous delirium — as when a virus attacks a healthy organism and overcomes it in the end. Gustave Le Bon, a French anthropologist and psychologist, tried to understand crowd behavior in his book *The Crowd: A Study of the Popular Mind*, published in 1895. Not coincidentally, Lenin, Stalin, and Hitler read Le Bon's work meticulously, focusing on the use of certain techniques of persuasion during their dictatorships. "Any lie, if repeated often, will transform gradually into the truth," Hitler maintained. Elias Canetti is illuminating as well in his work *Crowds and Power*, in which he highlights the mechanisms of the metamorphosis of the crowd that suddenly becomes anonymous, amorphous, and permeable and results in madness, always under a common leader who has a different name from one age to the next: Duce, Führer, Stalin, or even Xi Jinping. When people lose the principles of personal conscience and live ideologically, transgressing dangerous boundaries, they transform into and constitute the applauding basis of dictatorships. Ideologies are sick at the root. We believers are aware of our responsibility, of the primacy of conscience, of God, who loves all men, of the fact that our neighbor is our brother. We cannot justify wars of conquest against other countries or supremacy, as the Nazis did, according to a concept derived from biologism.

What do you think about Pius XII and his silence regarding Nazism? And how it was possible that after the publication of the drama* The Deputy *by Rolf Hochhuth, in the early 1970s, Pius XII was accused of Holocaust denial, whereas, after the war, even Golda Meir and the rabbi Isaac Herzog paid him homage?

When his silence is discussed, one detail often escapes most commentators. Eugenio Pacelli [Pius XII] spoke fluent German, and this enabled him to read, understand, and contextualize better than others what it meant to be a Catholic in Germany under Nazism. Considering how things went, I think it was a great injustice to have criticized him so bitterly, and especially in that way, after the publication of Hochhuth's theatrical work *The Deputy*. The criticisms were sparked by a wave of anti-Catholic propaganda nurtured by Communists toward the end of the 1960s. The Israeli prime minister Golda Meir praised Pius XII during a session of the United Nations, thanking him for what he did. It is true that during Hitler's dictatorship, the Holy See resolutely refused the anti-Catholic attitude of the Nazi regime, making use of the few diplomatic tools at his disposal at the time. They wanted to avoid public denouncements so as not to worsen the situation, sending it out of control. Their fears were quite real and concrete. The case of Holland had given cause to reflect. In 1941, the Nazis ordered a blanket sting operation in the convents where many Jews were being hidden after the denouncements against racial ideology made in the churches. Previously classified documents conserved in the Vatican archives are now coming out, and this is a good thing. Thanks to these papers, it will be possible to verify, confront, and certify the sequence of events. Patience is needed as historians finish this research to discover the truth from a broad perspective.

Pius XII sought to help persecuted Jews by every means at his disposal, and he chose not to condemn Hitler openly. He knew Germany well and was aware that he would never have been able to restrain the Nazi fury with an official stance. On the contrary, he was convinced that this would have ended in causing the deaths of many more people, adding evil to evil. The apostolic nunciatures in various occupied countries were immediately activated in giving shelter and aid to refugees. Within the Secretariat of State, a network was set up to offer information to those who needed it. The Vatican embassy in Budapest comes to mind. All of this was taking place in an oppressive setting, interwoven with suspicion and violence, in which many apostolic nuncios found it difficult to act. I think the decision to make the archives accessible, digitalizing them to show what truly happened, should be considered a service not only to the truth but to history as well, a worthy gesture toward Pius XII, a figure the Vatican would like to beatify. I, too, have nothing against this personally, although perhaps one ought to await the end of the historical investigations. It's a question of being patient a little longer.

You are very close to the workers' movement founded by Adolph Kolping (1813–1865), the Kolping Association, based on the idea of the Bishop Wilhelm von Ketteler of Mainz. Why is it so dear to you? Is there a personal or family connection?

From the Second Industrial Revolution, this social foundation has given assistance to the working classes of the Rhineland. My father was a laborer with Opel, working in a factory that originally produced wagons and later was transformed into an assembly line for vehicles fitted with wooden linings. He worked there until retirement. This is why I know that reality well and have close ties to it. It has been a great help to the working classes, educating them according to the social doctrine of the Church, emancipating them, helping them, and defending them.

What was your relationship with your father?

He was a serious man, the salt of the earth, honest, hardworking, and he did everything he could to support the family. He was not deluded with false hopes. He taught us to value respect for others, trust in providence, and the emotional well-being of the family. Every Sunday we went to Mass together.

My father's name was Martin, and he died in 1990; my mother's name was Lioba, and she passed away nine years later. I have warm memories of them, even though they were not effusive with us children; in those times, the emotional dynamics were focused on what was essential. Well, we Germans are not renowned for expressing emotions openly. My parents loved each other, of course, and respected each other, remaining always faithful, a tightly knit couple. I remember my father telling us that the best medicine against every form of stupidity was hard work. He had a preference for manual work and considered it a fundamental activity for his self-fulfillment. When I was in high school and he saw me hunched over my books all afternoon after attending classes all morning, he would make fun of me, saying that studies are not work at all. In any case, my dedication to studies derived from his example.

You live in the apartment that was Joseph Ratzinger's. Your home is also furnished from floor to ceiling with books. What do you recommend for someone wanting to know about Christianity?

[*A smile lights up Müller's face as he glances at the walls of volumes behind him and then turns his gaze to the walls next to him, also full of well-ordered books.*] Maybe St. Augustine, his *De Civitate Dei* [*City of God*]. Probably the center of it all, the source of understanding, remains the Bible because it contains the Word of God. Without Sacred Scripture, we just cannot go forward. I would also say there are other key texts that have accompanied the two thousand years of Christian thought, but they come after. Those who have not studied theology and want to deepen their understanding can consult Joseph Ratzinger's *Introduction to Christianity* — truly fundamental. Then there are the works of Yves Congar, Hans Urs von Balthasar, Karl Rahner, the Church Fathers, St. Gregory the Great, St. Thomas, Duns Scotus, St. Bonaventure. I could continue this list at length.

You worked at the Congregation for the Doctrine of the Faith, and then, inexplicably in 2017, you were removed from the post five years early (in general, one retires at seventy-five in the Curia). Regarding Pope

Francis's decision, what weight was given to your reservations regarding **Amoris Laetitia,** *the post-synodal exhortation that opened the path to divorced and remarried couples' reception of Communion?*

My departure occurred in 2017. It was completely out of the blue. The previous day was June 29, the solemnity of Peter and Paul, and I recall how Pope Francis embraced me in the sanctuary of the basilica in front of everyone at the end of Mass, telling me how he had complete confidence in me. That's exactly what he said. The next day, I went punctually to the apostolic palace in audience to present him with a series of pending issues, a routine appointment for the prefect of the Congregation for the Doctrine of the Faith. At the conclusion of this brief meeting, he told me in a summary way, "Your term is over. Thank you for your work" — without offering any reasons. But as it turned out, he never offered any later either. He merely added that he had found some other task to entrust to me after the summer of that year. Since then, nothing has transpired. I still recall that moment vividly because it was so unexpected. Although surprised, I answered him that when I came to Rome in 2012, I had left behind a tenured university chair that I loved and a large diocese in Germany, and I had no aspiration to pursue a career in the Roman Curia. I came to the Vatican purely out of obedience to the call of Benedict XVI, who wanted me by his side for my theological competence, as he had often explained. I added that, for me, it was a service and that if his desire was to send me away, I would have gone immediately. I told him as well that I had other tasks to perform and that he need not concern himself with me.

Was Pope Francis uncomfortable when he communicated that measure to you?

I wouldn't say uncomfortable. Rather, it was his satisfied countenance that struck me. Sometime later I found out that immediately after our meeting, practically as soon as I had left the room, the pope grabbed the phone and called the Jesuit Luis Francisco Ladaria, the cardinal who was then nominated prefect of the Congregation for the Doctrine of the Faith in my place. The pope told Ladaria that he was satisfied with how he had handled the situation and had made me hand in my resignation, adding that the path was clear for giving the office to Ladaria. I am convinced he thought of this step at least two weeks beforehand, when I knew nothing of it. No one had ever mentioned anything of the sort to me. But it was all prepared, even the press release publicized with great fanfare.

I reflected quite a bit over this hasty style, and perhaps I was not even surprised because there had already been precedents. At the Congregation for the Doctrine of the Faith, for example, several priests had been dismissed in similar fashion by the pope sometime before that — fired without justification. I recall having defended them, going to Santa Marta[2] on their behalf to try to change Francis's mind, but it was to no avail. He was inflexible and would hear none of it. Unfortunately, this way of doing things has caused a lot of concern within the Vatican in recent years. With some of those who were dismissed from their positions in the same way, it has been my fate to explain that no one can question the pontiff, and I have tried to reason with those experiencing a bit of anger and filling the ranks of an internal opposition. The good of the Church must always prevail, it seems to me. That is an absolute principle.

One should always tend toward the defense of unity. In the case of my departure, I discovered that at the root of it, there had been a series of complaints about me because of my doctrinal rigor and because I am a theologian and, moreover, German. It seems paradoxical, but that's how it is. They saw me as the rigid German professor who wanted to

---

[2]   Santa Marta is the residence of Pope Francis.

lecture even the pope, but it was all false, a big exaggeration. I was just defending the rules. More simply put, I suppose the pope had cultivated over time a form of diffidence, an aversion, toward theologians, German university scholars. I am sure that it's something that dates back to the period when, as a young Jesuit, he lived in Germany while finishing his studies.

The task of the prefect of the Congregation for the Doctrine of the Faith, however, is to assist the Successor of Peter, to show him the way, to collaborate with him while keeping his gaze fixed on doctrine, even at the cost of raising questions about the risk of possible doctrinal errors in this or that document or in the face of weak argumentation that needs to be strengthened or deepened. This obviously does not mean being disloyal or dissenting. Even the great theologian Robert Bellarmine was dismissed twice from the Roman Curia because of disagreements with the pope. There is no infidelity whatsoever in this; if anything, it is collaboration with and loyalty to the Church, her history, and her doctrine.

Have you heard from Francis in these past years?

He sent me a note when he learned of my brother's fatal accident. Then later, in February of 2022, he sent me another message in which he recognized the merits of my theological journey and asked me to write a book on the various expressions of Gnosticism pervading our society.

What might be the cause of your sudden and even traumatic dismissal, besides the perplexity you expressed over Amoris Laetitia, seeing how you never received a thorough justification?

Three years before my resignation, as Massimo Franco recalled in his book *The Monastery*, the pope had an illuminating dialogue with his friend the Argentinian theologian Víctor Manuel Fernández, of Buenos Aires, who spoke to him openly of the need (for the pontiff) to send me home because, as he explained in the interview, I corrected the pope, evidently considering myself superior to him. The verdict was clear. The sentence is self-explanatory, and it amazed me, since I had served Bergoglio's pontificate loyally. It seems some Latin American theologians have never stopped suffering from a poorly concealed inferiority complex, esteeming European theologians as old carcasses, a bit medieval, dusty, and even obsolete.

The approach of many (obviously not all) Latin American theologians is to concentrate on the primacy of pastoral activity in the modern world, compared with the vision of European theologians, more focused on rules. During my life, however, I have had the good fortune of working with the theologian Gustavo Gutiérrez, one of the founders of Liberation Theology. I spent at least two months a year in Peru and Brazil, living and working in the immense favelas and teaching in seminaries and parishes in the hinterland.

But perhaps there is more to it. It is difficult to forget another episode that might clarify the matter. After the election of Pope Francis, the Honduran cardinal Óscar Maradiaga, one of the main electors, expressed harsh criticism for my theological Weltanschauung, explaining in public that the prefect of the Congregation for the Doctrine of the Faith was the classic German professor, incapable of interpreting the true reality of people. In this context as well, one glimpses the usual Latin American prejudice toward European theologians. In any case, my defense of theological rigor was not appreciated, at least in those forms.

I remember another occasion when I published in *L'Osservatore Romano* a detailed article on the indissolubility of marriage. In short order, I received a phone call from Andrea Tornielli, an Italian journalist and friend of the pope. At the time, he had not yet entered the Vatican Dicastery for Communication. He contacted me to let me know that the theological tack I had expressed in the text published on *Amoris Laetitia* was certainly not the same as Pope Francis's. He wanted to know from me whether the pontiff had given me permission to write it. In effect, he was asking if I had been authorized to publish in *L'Osservatore Romano*. I was stunned by the obtuse questions because anyone could have understood that the text was a contribution to an ongoing debate and that the prefect of the Congregation for the Doctrine of the Faith had the duty to analyze and develop the theological line of the Magisterium. But for the theologians of the papal circle, I remained too dangerously close to the line of Ratzinger. And I must say that every so often at the congregation, I happened to read downright heresies.

What are you referring to?

Once, the Argentinian theologian Víctor Manuel Fernández stated that, in the future, the Apostolic See could be moved to any other part of the world — for example, to a Latin American city such as Buenos Aires, Rio de Janeiro, or Montevideo. This is obviously an absurd proposal. The papacy is located geographically and historically in Rome not by chance or caprice but because the bishop of Rome resides there, and he is the Successor of Peter. And as such, he cannot have another seat, such as New York or Brasilia or Milan. The *Cathedra Petri* can be only in Rome. Furthermore, the Catholic Church, being a *communio ecclesiarum*, elects the pontiff and no other bishop in the world. The apostles Peter and Paul went to Rome, where they suffered martyrdom, and already from St. Irenaeus of Lyon (we're in the second century AD), one spoke of the Petrine primacy because all had to flow into the Church of Rome. And this was not because it was the capital of the Roman Empire but because its holy patrons were martyred and buried there.

One day, I raised the issue directly with the pontiff, explaining that no authority could move the *Cathedra Petri* to another place. He said nothing. Today in the *Annuario Pontificio*, however, in the first few pages, where the pontiff's titles are printed, it is specified that *Vicar of Christ* and *Successor of Peter* are merely historical titles! And yet the constitution *Lumen Gentium*, regarding the sequence of titles, is very precise in affirming, for example, that the bishop of Rome is also the Vicar of Christ and the Successor of the Apostles. These are, in fact, dogmatic titles that cannot be lowered or reduced. These are not details. The historical title *Primate of Italy* came only much later. At the root of the modifications Francis brought to the *Annuario Pontificio*, I see a latent form of negation of the Petrine foundation of the papacy. There are some things that just do not add up anymore.

For example?

For starters, a lot of work is being done on decentralization, but at the same time, on the other side, they are reinforcing the centering base. I'll give you an example, the most recent. The priestly Ordination of four future presbyters was prohibited in Toulon, France. The order to block everything came from Rome, despite the fact that Ordination is an act that falls under the tasks of any diocesan bishop and, as such, there was no need whatsoever for a similar intervention by the central authority. In the Diocese of Toulon, the future priests were halted because they belonged to the category of conservatives. I do not know if there were other problems behind this, but someone in Rome decided it was necessary to impose the ban. I underline the episode to show that, if, on one hand, the pope is working on the organizational architecture aimed at decentralizing ecclesiastical structures, on the other, decisions have been centralized that belong, by rule, to diocesan bishops in their jurisdiction, which derives from the sacrament of Ordination and, therefore, from Christ. It is evident that we cannot speak of a "dictatorship," as was said in several books quite critical of Pope Francis. Nevertheless, one cannot be silent on the effects produced by certain tendencies. Many of these positions have been suggested to the pope by some of his closest advisers. There is a sort of magical circle that gravitates around Santa Marta, formed by people who, in my opinion, are not theologically prepared.

Another emblematic episode was reported in the news and concerns an ex–interior minister of Italy, Marco Minniti. During a closed-door meeting of the Italian Episcopal Conference in May 2022, Pope Francis described him as if he were a criminal of war for having signed the diplomatic accord with Libya, which resulted in terrifying refugee camps in which thousands of migrants were tortured. Early in 2022, Minniti had been invited to Florence for a convention promoted by the Italian bishops and the mayor. Pope Francis was expected to attend as well, but once he learned that he would have to encounter the ex-minister (whom the pope considered responsible for the disastrous immigration policy in Libya), he canceled at the last moment. He did not show up in Florence, just to avoid a diplomatic incident. Nor did he send greetings to the convention that Sunday during the Angelus, despite the presence there of the president of the Italian Republic. In this case as well, one might ask who informed the pope or what they did to provoke such a reaction?

In the Vatican, it seems that information circulates on parallel planes. On one side, the institutional channels are active, though less frequently consulted by the pontiff, unfortunately. On the other side, there are his personal channels, used even for the nomination of bishops and cardinals. At times, it happens that the regular investigations into candidates for the episcopate or the cardinalate are put aside in favor of the discretional procedure of certain nominations suggested by the usual "magical circle" that evidently exercises a great influence over the pope, despite the risk of derailing him, as has happened in some circumstances.

What did you think of the court case of Cardinal Angelo Becciu, who was punished by Pope Francis before being condemned? Why was the presumption of innocence not applied?

You cannot punish someone without having proof of guilt in hand. This way of acting is frequent in the Vatican and concerns not only the individual case of Becciu but has happened even within the Congregation for the Doctrine of the Faith, when several priests were sent away without reason. For Cardinal Becciu, the question was amplified by the mass media: he was humiliated and punished before the world without being given any possibility to defend himself. We now await the end of the trial underway in the Vatican tribunal. And yet the presumption of innocence should be given to anyone; it has been a sacrosanct right since the times of the ancient Romans. I do not intend to spin diatribes in this regard, but it's difficult not to be amazed by how the entire affair has developed: Francis decided to punish him severely after someone went to him in Santa Marta and showed him an article from *L'Espresso*, an Italian weekly, that ran an investigation of the cardinal. But how can you act on the basis of a news article?

Personally, I am not in favor of holding civil trials in the Vatican; better that they be done in Italy with Italian or European procedures, because the Vatican is not a state like others, having been created solely to guarantee the independence of the person of the pope. We do not even have our own population in this little territory of barely forty-four hectares.[3] In any case, beyond my personal considerations, punishing

---

[3] The Vatican State measures forty-four square hectares, not forty-four square kilometers, as stated in the original text. — Trans.

someone before he is sentenced points to the blind power of an absolute monarch, a sort of artifact of the pope-king, despite the Church's having liberated herself long ago of the Papal States. As concerns the trial about the London apartment development, I do not know the exact terms. I hope, as everyone does, that light will be shed on the matter. Judging from the standpoint of the prosecutorial system, it would seem that all functionaries living in the Vatican are corrupt to the bone — a prejudice that ought to be dismantled. That's not exactly how things are. Naturally, any guilty party should be punished, but after regular sentencing.

Why has the College of Cardinals not yet intervened publicly in Becciu's case?

The College of Cardinals cannot act without or against the pope. It is not an autonomous entity. For seven years, a consistory had not been convoked to examine the issues facing the Church, as would have been the proper custom. But the cardinals could not convoke themselves and freely discuss matters; they had to wait until the pope did so. But for a long time, Francis considered this unnecessary, whereas, in the past, it took place regularly, at least once a year. In August 2022, a consistory was convoked, although without discussing the Becciu case nor even the case of Joseph Zen Ze-kiun, the cardinal emeritus of Hong Kong, currently on trial after being accused by the Chinese authorities for having defended human rights and democratic principles. Zen, too, is suffering inexplicable treatment. He has asked repeatedly to speak with Francis about the issue of Hong Kong and China, but he has never been received in Santa Marta. I remember that when he arrived in Rome, after making the long journey at eighty years of age, he waited a number of days in his hotel, hoping to receive a call from the pope's secretary so that he could be received. But it never came, and so he returned to Hong Kong a few days later. A humiliation.

Perhaps if we really want to reform the Church, we cardinals should start with ourselves and learn to act on gospel principles, without fear of speaking openly. It's not about criticizing the pontiff but about confronting the circumstantial reality, in a collegial way, for the good of the unity of the Church. It's not a matter of partisan conduct as if we were Guelphs and Ghibellines all over again. But if something is not working, what is needed is for us to take courage and together, as brothers, to find a synthesis.

Catherine of Siena left us a great teaching: she had very strong words against the popes but never against the papacy as an institution. And it is obvious as well that the pontiff, as a man, is not perfect. So if there are matters to denounce in order to improve the overall situation, the only path is to speak openly. "Let what you say be simply 'Yes' or 'No'; anything more than this comes from evil" (Matt. 5:37). The Church must always fight for values, for human rights — a field in which she was working long before many international treaties. We do not preach the gospel because we have signed a treaty; we must preach the truth because it is inscribed in the divine law and in natural law. The Church cannot act like some sort of corporation, a multinational, but as a reality that imitates Christ and is called to be coherent in every way.

After eight years in the works, the apostolic constitution **Praedicate Evangelium** *was published on March 19, 2022, and it redesigns the map of power in the Curia through an important plan of reform. A significant decentralization is foreseen, with fewer functions for the Secretariat of State and greater weight for the Congregation for the Evangelization of Peoples (thus becoming the most important dicastery), while the Congregation for the Doctrine of the Faith loses the historical weight it once enjoyed. The aim is to move to another stage in the realization* *of the Church of the periphery. Does this change in pace mean giving less importance to doctrine than the Church had always given before?*

The constitution required years of preparation, although, in my view, it ends up lacking a coherent ecclesiological vision. What jumps out immediately when one reads it is that the Roman Curia has been reduced to a corporation that gives assistance to its "clients," the bishops' conferences, as if it were a multinational and no longer an ecclesiastical body. Both historically and symbolically, the Curia ought to have as its load-bearing column the College of Cardinals, a key body that represents the Roman Church in its entirety and possesses primacy, next to the pope. It is not incidental that when a pontiff dies, it is precisely the Roman Church — namely, the cardinals — that administers the primacy.

The very title of the constitutional text seems misleading to me: *Praedicate Evangelium*, "preach the gospel," is not a prerogative of the Curia. It is the task of each of the faithful. Whoever wrote it seems to have thought that the activity of evangelization was the most important of the Faith. Naturally, this is not the case: evangelization is very relevant in the world, very important, but an upheaval of this proportion was not necessary because the proclamation of the gospel for the conversion of non-Christians does not begin with the Curia or the Roman Church. It is, if anything, an ordinary task for all local churches, and it is the pontiff's task to unite the faithful in faith in Jesus — no light task, it seems to me. To the contrary.

The safeguarding of the Faith is the foundation of everything. The conciliar constitution *Lumen Gentium*, in paragraph 23, clarifies this point:

> This collegial union is apparent also in the mutual relations of the individual bishops with particular churches and with the universal Church. The Roman Pontiff, as the successor of Peter, is the

perpetual and visible principle and foundation of unity of both the bishops and of the faithful. The individual bishops, however, are the visible principle and foundation of unity in their particular churches, fashioned after the model of the universal Church, in and from which churches comes into being the one and only Catholic Church. For this reason individual bishops represent each his own church, but all of them together and with the Pope represent the entire Church in the bond of peace, love and unity.

If the final text does not reflect the line of tradition, how was it possible to come to an overturning of the perspective of the safekeeping of the Faith in favor of evangelization?

I think that among the collaborators who accompanied Pope Francis on this long journey of elaboration, there was an insufficient presence of theologians. It seems to me the most critical point. Even the foundations of *Lumen Gentium*, a conciliar constitution of crucial importance for the Church, which indicates how to develop the theological and ecclesiological character of the College of Cardinals, were lost along the way. The idea advanced and carried out by the pope, on the other hand, points in the opposite direction. The Roman Curia is not any mere government administration. It is an apparatus created and inspired by *communio ecclesiarum*; in the same way, the bishops are not simple functionaries. Unfortunately, the constitution *Praedicate Evangelium* was born with a birth defect, an initial prejudice that asserted itself during the conclave that elected Pope Francis: I am referring to anti-Roman sentiment and bias. From the very beginning, the Latin American cardinals insisted on this aspect and planned to build a Church in their own image — to a certain extent, a bit partisan — based on their vision of the world. The reform of the Curia is theorized without taking into account the historical and symbolic role of the Curia.

The concept of the Church established by *Lumen Gentium* revolves around the *unitas ecclesiarum*, whereas now a form of decentralization is being carried out that is inspired by administrative and political dynamics that give more power to the bishops' conferences. To avoid this macroscopic error, it would have sufficed to answer a simple question: Who (and what) can give power to whom? The answer is that even the pope cannot give power to the bishops, given that, at the moment of consecration, they receive it directly from the Holy Spirit through the sacrament of Ordination. The bishops are united to the pope, and each of them acts with his own power, received by means of the sacrament. This indicates that from a theological point of view, a pope is not the owner of the Church or her CEO or the lead shareholder. All authority in the Church descends from the Holy Spirit by means of the sacrament. As for the bishops, obviously they are not like apostolic nuncios, ambassadors to the Holy See who depend instead on the pope. It is for this reason that the pope cannot remove from office or banish a bishop just because that bishop no longer pleases him. Yet this happened even in Italy: I know of a bishop who was sent away simply because he expressed dissent over some anti-Covid measures imposed by the Italian government during the lockdowns. The pope should not have been able to dismiss him.

Which bishop was that?

I remember that, despite having no issues with the Italian government at that time, this bishop was forced to resign. It happened in a diocese in central Italy.[4] It was an incomprehensible action. Naturally, a pope can dismiss a bishop if he acts contrary to the Catholic Faith

---

[4]   Msgr. Giovanni D'Ercole, former bishop of Ascoli Piceno, resigned on October 29, 2020.

or destroys the unity of the Church but certainly not for cultivating a differing opinion on other matters. Bishops are not required to give total obedience as if to a dictator. The respect of obedience exists but on matters linked to the Faith. It's not a sporting event in which bishops are fans for this team or that team. Here, too, in my opinion, the lack of solid theological foundation can be felt.

And yet the text of Praedicate Evangelium made use of great canonists such as Fr. Gianfranco Ghirlanda, who is now a cardinal.

Fr. Ghirlanda, whom I highly esteem, proposes a juridical vision shared by other canonists that is based, primarily, on the jurisdictional power of the pontiff, which basically means that the pope, above and beyond the ordained bishop, has full *potestas*. Too bad it's not that way. His *potestas* is over the universal Church, not over the single churches. The difference is the jurisdiction between the pope and the bishops. In effect, this tendency distinguishes *ius divinum* from the sacramentality of the Church, despite the fact that, as we said before, the Second Vatican Council overcame this dilemma some time ago.

What do you expect from the application of this constitution?

To be honest, I don't expect much. It all depends on whether they will be able to reformulate the text in the future and, hopefully, develop it better theologically. From the published structure, there transpires the intention to give the Curia the typical layout of a civil organization in which every aspect is heavily controlled, with disciplinary surveillance in the background to avoid abuses of power, corruption, and so forth. A layman or a priest who enters the Curia to work is expected to possess a consonant mentality oriented toward serving the Church, regardless of the existing norms in place. Such persons ought to be Christians with a proven faith, at every level. In this new outlook, however, the spiritual aspect is diminished, no longer important, whereas external controls (the auditors) rise in the ranks. And then, let me make an analysis that is quite harsh, generally speaking.

Namely?

After the Council of Trent, too, it was considered necessary to optimize the state of the Curia. What did they do to improve things? Simple. They nominated good priests, bishops, and cardinals: Bellarmine, Borromeo, and also St. Philip Neri, a legendary parish priest, practically Rome's second apostle. They were of the opinion that conciliar decrees and juridical formulas would not have sufficed if not supported by people of an elevated intellectual, human, and moral caliber, capable of applying the norms and making them known in heart and mind. I wonder what progress can be made in the Church by all these new documents and restructurings if, at the base, we lack people with a recognized intellectual and spiritual depth. Naturally, it would be unrealistic to imagine that all who offer their service to the Curia are saints with halos over their heads; it would be improbable. It is, after all, a human organization, and every one of us is a sinner. One must presume, however, that people are motivated by goodwill to work for the Church without seeking their own interests, without jostling to advance their career, without nepotism, and without influence peddling. Jesus gave His life for us all — not, of course, to seek His own personal interests.

You are using very strong words regarding the new constitution. Are you perhaps asking for modifications to the text?

The consistory convoked for the end of August 2022, alas, arrived too late. I wonder what we cardinals could have discussed. The text had already

been released and approved. At this point, whoever raises constructive criticism gets accused of offering opposition, of being an enemy of
Francis — exactly as happened already with the publication of *Amoris
Laetitia*. Whoever criticizes the text, or might do so in the future, will
automatically be added to the list of the pope's enemies — even if they
obviously are not. Discussion would certainly have been positive, constructive, and useful, but it should have come before. Perhaps it is no
coincidence that there were no consistories; for years the convocation
did not come. I don't think it makes any sense to discuss the matter now
under present conditions. It seems Francis is inclined to implement, align,
control, and flatten. I would like to strike up debate over the theological
and ecclesiological conception of the text, but by now it's useless.

What other points in the text are problematic?

There are a number of critical points. One aspect that struck me was
the absurd choice not to use the name *congregation*: in the final text,
the use of the word *dicastery* prevailed. Words are important. Perhaps
some research into the origin of the appellation *congregation* would have
been useful because it meant a little consistory up until the sixteenth
century. They were the consistories of all the cardinals. *Dicastery* is
merely a technical term borrowed from the old Byzantine Empire,
where there were *ministerium* of the state. *Congregation*, however, has a
theological root. *Synod* is the Greek word for the Latin corresponding
to *congregation*: *congregatio*. It all sounds so incoherent to me. Or there
might be another explanation — that perhaps whoever redacted the
text is master of neither Latin nor Greek [*laughs heartily*].

But the text revolves around the concept of synodality, which seems to me much more important.

By now, the term *synodality* has become a passe-partout, used everywhere. With this new constitution, the Curia is concentrated on the pope as a person, even though the pope cannot change the divine conception of the Church. Episcopal collegiality is per se the synod of bishops. Take, for example, the Synod on Synodality convoked by Francis in 2021: the bishops are already the heads of the local churches with the specific task of guiding the Church of Christ according to grace and not according to the rules of some political power. Furthermore, a synod of bishops already existed. A de facto democratization, or protestantizing, is underway, in my opinion.

Because I am a German, my thoughts turn immediately to what is happening in Germany, where, in 2019, with the approval of Rome, a synodal way was opened from which rather cheeky critiques and unsustainable theological requests are emerging. In this framework, there are even those who would like to exercise control from below over the election of bishops, even though, for the Church, it is not a matter of designating just any person, a functionary or a bureaucrat, or electing a bishop as if he were the governor of a state tied to the will of the people, precisely as a representative. This sort of representative and majority-rule mechanism has little to do with the Church. A bishop is ordained by the Holy Spirit and receives a mandate. St. Paul left us a very important passage: "No man made me an apostle" (see Gal. 1:1). In the debates in Germany, in the documents published, and in the exchanges taking place, too little is said of God, Christ, grace, and truth. The exercise of power, rather, is heatedly discussed.

The Abuse Scandals

Germany, like every country in the world, has been affected by the sexual abuse scandals. When you were bishop of the Diocese of Regensburg, did you ever have to confront cases of pedophilia? Did you ever cover them up?

The problem began to be seriously discussed in Germany twenty years ago, although only in 2010 did the issue become quite intense, under the pressure of public opinion. Before then, there were almost no investigations in the dioceses. I, too, found myself having to manage several cases, with the help of my expert collaborators, and I did so by faithfully following the *Code of Canon Law*. When the first numbers of victims began to be released on the national level, I was shocked. I had never had the impression of a phenomenon of this type because nothing had ever happened near me, despite my having been in contact with scores of priests during my life, from the seminary to every other priestly setting. The effect of this wound on people is terrible. I ask myself how a priest consecrated to God can prey on minors, teenagers, condemning them to enormous psychological trauma. This is not only a question of grave sin but an abominable crime against the person.

In February 2022, Joseph Ratzinger took pen and paper and responded to those who accused him, after the Munich Report, of having covered up a pedophile while still bishop of the Bavarian diocese in the 1980s. In one passage in the letter, he writes that he understands perfectly "the repulsion and the fear that Christ experienced on the Mount of Olives when He saw interiorly all the terrible things He would have to overcome." Ratzinger then adds an image: "That moment when the disciples were sleeping unfortunately represents the situation that once again has become a reality today and for which I, too, feel invited to participate. Thus, I can only pray the Lord and supplicate all the angels and saints and you, dear brothers and sister, to pray for me." It is a meditated letter in which he asks forgiveness, enlarging the field of vision. When he underlines that all were sleeping like the disciples, what does he mean?

Not only did Ratzinger exonerate himself after the problem erupted, but he did much more; he admitted that in the Church, over many years before this terrible wound, there had not been the necessary vigilance — to the point where everyone was slumbering (I use this word *slumbering* on purpose), as the apostles were. In effect, they failed to act in the face of evil. When Ratzinger says "all" in the letter, he implicitly includes himself as well. He excludes no one. This means there was an erroneous mentality. The idea I have developed, personally collecting information from the Munich investigations, is that it was an instrument of propaganda to weaken the image of the pope emeritus in Germany. Ratzinger represents a symbol; he incarnates the part of the German Church most faithful to the Magisterium and therefore least inclined to give ground under the blows of the reforms that the promoters of the synodal way are advancing.

Beyond this (although it might seem marginal), it must be said that, regarding the abuse scandals, the past twenty years have seen the fortunate maturation of a culture more sensitive to this drama. Today, we all perceive immediately the suffering in the victims' faces, an aspect that was previously neglected. Up until the American scandal, the prevailing tendency was to correct the priests who had abused or molested, without examining with due attention the victims' perspective, taking upon us the weight of their pain. At times, we did not punish those who had committed abominable actions, and we were not concerned about those who had suffered shameful actions with so much pain and suffering. The change of perspective that has matured in the Church is precisely this. I find it shocking that a pastor consecrated to God could destroy a fragile person, a handicapped person, or a child for sexual aims. We know well that in other areas of society, there are high percentages of abuse, that pedophilia lurks in families, in sporting and scholastic settings; nonetheless, for a priest, a minister of God, it remains something twice as grave.

This theme has been a source of concern, painful decisions, lacerations for decades. In March 2017, you were widely contested by Marie Collins, a victim of an Irish priest when she was an adolescent. She accused you of being a liar because the Pontifical Commission for the Protection of Minors, of which Collins was a member at the time, stated that it was you who did not want to shed light on the bishops' protectors, those who had preferred to conceal the pedophiles and not the victims. The storm broke over the case of the Chilean bishop Barros, accused of having hidden horrific cases. Within the Congregation for the Doctrine of the Faith, why was it so difficult to shed light on the responsibility of the bishops?

I would like to begin with a reflection on the controversy initiated by Ms. Collins, a woman whom I consider courageous and appreciate for being rigorous with herself and others. I remember well when she addressed those unjust accusations against me. They were the fruit of a partial vision of how the Roman Curia works and its normative procedures. Obviously, Collins was speaking as a victim, weighed down by pain and her desire for justice, without knowing how the various congregations intervene in such cases. The theme of negligent bishops falls under the authority of the Dicastery of Bishops and, if action is not initiated there, it is not possible to proceed elsewhere. In 2019, Pope Francis published a motu proprio, *Vos Estis Lux Mundi*, in which he reorganized the jurisdictions of the Vatican dicasteries. At the Congregation for the Doctrine of the Faith, there exists a functioning tribunal that can be activated when charges are filed on *delicta graviora*, the more serious crimes. I have never spoken personally with Ms. Collins; I would have liked to converse with her. It would have been productive, and I could have illustrated to her the state of things. We could have collaborated. I was sorry to hear her call me a liar, and I don't even know why she did so.

As concerns the Barros case, I could not have acted on it anyway. I remember that the pontifical commission on abuse had made the proposal that the Congregation for the Doctrine of the Faith should establish the punishments for negligent bishops, forgetting, however, that the internal constitutional norms regarding the functioning of the Curia ought to have been modified. I was not the one to change them. In the end, a fruitless and somewhat senseless media diatribe was instigated between me and Ms. Collins. Pope Francis never wanted to support the proposal of the Pontifical Commission for the Protection of Minors. At the time, he limited himself to saying that he would evaluate it, and then everything ended up on a shelf. It was in that context that Ms. Collins reported that it had been Cardinal Müller who had rejected the idea, but that is not how it happened. Other cardinals later affirmed that the judgment upon the bishops' conduct had to remain in the canonical context, as was already provided for in the *Code of Canon Law*.

Marie Collins went away slamming the door. Then, however, in the new organization foreseen by the apostolic constitution **Praedicate**

Evangelium, *the Pontifical Commission for the Protection of Minors was permanently inserted into the Congregation for the Doctrine of the Faith. This was the result of the reform that came into effect in June 2022. In the end, Collins was right, and her idea was developed, to the point of becoming an integral part of the dicastery that safeguards doctrine.*

The Pontifical Commission for the Protection of Minors became part of the Congregation for the Doctrine of the Faith, although it remains an independent organization of an advisory nature. It can use the terrain and the instruments, but it cannot access canonical trials because this organism is not part of the internal tribunal, at least according to current regulations. It has the power to advise, to draft reports, to make evaluations that guide episcopal conferences with the aim of raising the level of prevention against sexual abuse. Perhaps when she was nominated, Ms. Collins imagined that she had to oversee everything, but obviously this was not possible because the commission was not equipped with the necessary normative instruments. During my mandate at the Congregation for the Doctrine of the Faith, we continued to work according to existing regulations and could not have done otherwise. Our collaborators always acted in good faith, within the normative framework. I was so sorry for this quarrel, the fruit of an incomplete perspective.

Why is there so little transparency at the Congregation for the Doctrine of the Faith? For example, why not publish statistics periodically, or why not disclose the verdicts regarding pedophile priests?

In the absence of modifications to the internal regulations, the congregation must send the rulings to the bishops, and it is up to their discretion — because it is in their jurisdiction — to make them public or not, as well as to disclose the sentences imposed in the trials. As for statistics on abuse, in reality they exist and are collected but only for internal use, without any external divulgation foreseen. The decision to make them public does not depend on the prefect of the dicastery. I'm not sure if it's a question of limited transparency; those are the rules. What is certain is that a dicastery cannot wake up one morning and act in a way that transgresses the regulations in force. The authority for changing, in the final analysis, lies in the hands of the pontiff, who can decide whatever he considers opportune. The congregation and the other curial realities exist only to assist the governance of the pope and the bishops.

If I'm not mistaken, we did publish some statistics on priests reduced to the lay state. Eighty-five percent of the victims were males. Perhaps in the future, on the basis of matured experience, everything ought to be rendered more transparent. The program regarding abuse can always be revised considering that, in the Vatican, the norms are quite strict. In effect, the procedures can be improved.

Staying on the theme of the lack of transparency, the case of the Argentine bishop Gustavo Zanchetta has raised a lot of questions in recent years, as he is a dear friend of the pope and was accused and convicted of abuse. Several years ago, he was called to the Vatican just when the judicial tempest that was to come down upon him was raging. The pope created a special role at APSA, the Holy See's Patrimony Administration. The bishop is now under house arrest in Argentina. At the Congregation for the Doctrine of the Faith, a canonical trial was opened, although nothing is known about its progress or the bishop's sentence. Why so much mystery?

A canonical trial was conducted for his case, although I do not know the results. Zanchetta is the subject of much discussion because of his privileged status as a friend of the pope. Friendship should not, as a rule, influence the legal process; all must be treated in the same way. This is the problem, also because the pope, with his authority, can suspend a trial.

While I was in charge of the Congregation for the Doctrine of the Faith, an interesting case occurred, that of Fr. Mauro Inzoli, a priest connected with Communion and Liberation. The Vatican tribunal tried him and, in the end, decided to reduce him to the lay state because he was found guilty of crimes. Unfortunately, however, a cardinal in the Curia went knocking on the door of Santa Marta, asking for clemency. In the face of this interference, the pope was swayed and chose to modify the verdict, changing Inzoli's sentence, allowing him to remain a cleric but forbidding him to wear clerical garb in public and to present himself as a consecrated man in communities. He remained consecrated but could not show himself to others as such.

This is only one example, but I remember several cardinals who reacted in a quite contrary way to the sentence of being reduced to the lay state for clergy guilty of abuse. They exercised pressure to overturn the decisions in their zeal for the defense of civil liberties, stating that to deprive a priest of his sacerdotal status was the equivalent of a death sentence. And given that the death sentence was deleted from the *Catechism of the Catholic Church*, it would be an inconsistency to carry it out in other circumstances. That is what happened to Polish, American, and other foreign clergy condemned by the tribunal of the Congregation for the Doctrine of the Faith. Their sentencing proceeded swiftly to their reduction from the clerical state, whereas for Italian priests, the application of their sentence was carried out with great difficulty because, behind the scenes, influential friends knocked on the door at Santa Marta, asking the pope to intercede. And in the end, they almost always succeeded.

Was it for this reason they introduced a revision entity to evaluate the most serious sentences?

In 2014, the pope instituted at the Congregation for the Doctrine of the Faith the college for the revision of these trials. Composed of seven bishops, this organism can even overturn the verdicts of the tribunal and impede the defrocking of priests. I was never pleased about this trend; I complained dozens of times, but many in the Vatican had very different ideas. Ultimately, I ended up branded as the rigid German theologian always wanting to apply the rules in an inflexible manner. But if the tribunal of the congregation found a priest guilty of committing a grave crime against a minor, obviously his dismissal from the clerical state would be due. In the Roman Curia, however, there are still some who exert pressure on the pope, and when I was prefect, they added in support that Cardinal Müller was excessively harsh, to the detriment of mercy. Yet still, in the face of such horrible things, one cannot give in; it's not a question of being harsh or less harsh but of being impartial and exercising justice. Cardinal Angelo Sodano, now deceased, was always one of those champion-of-civil-liberties cardinals who never wanted to expose clerics by virtue of their sacred orders. It may be that Cardinal Sodano could not or did not want to give credit to those horrible accusations. On the contrary, Cardinal Ratzinger, as prefect of the Congregation for the Doctrine of the Faith, held a completely opposite opinion.

Two lines of action have always existed in the Vatican. One line is inclined toward maximum rigor and the other toward finding an indulgent course of action capable of mitigating the punishment of the guilty cleric. The college for revision almost always succeeded in canceling the sentences delivered. The archbishop Charles Scicluna — now the head of this college — is a man of exceptional rigor, and I hope he will be able to find a clear and just line. Still, I ask: Can there ever exist an independent college within the Congregation for the Doctrine of the Faith? The existence of an administrative body of that type risks creating divisions.

What do you think of the independent national commissions promoted by many governments to analyze the scourge of sexual abuse?

I am in favor if the matter is studied in its entirety, though one should avoid the coarse errors committed in France, where the independent commission is designated CIASE[5] and is approved by the episcopate. The initiative was sharply attacked for the criteria applied in the research and the statistics it used. Perhaps they should have been completed before being applied. The result is an abnormal, exaggerated number of victims, evidently padded. You can see it immediately. A complete analysis requires rules, competent people, and nonideological dynamics. Personally, I am not in favor of royal commissions that often give the impression of having been created by governments with the sole aim of crippling the Church and not really of analyzing an aberrant phenomenon to be stamped out. This phenomenon concerns just a minority and not the totality of clergy, and as such, it should be framed in a constructive way and taken up with a view to justice for the good of minors and of society.

[5] Independent Commission on Sexual Abuse in the Church.

The Rift

In the past few years in Rome, a rift with "traditionalists" has opened up. Benedict XVI succeeded in finding a path that would have guaranteed, over time, their integration. The decisions made by Francis to prohibit the Mass in Latin have put everything up in the air once more. The Latin Mass with the priest facing the altar can no longer be celebrated in parish churches, except for in extraordinary cases authorized by the diocesan bishop. Why give so much weight to a prohibition that seems almost marginal?

The so-called traditionalists, it must be said, are not a homogenous group, as some might think. There are various realities that reject and vigorously oppose the Second Vatican Council; they consider themselves not aligned with conciliar doctrine. These groups are effectively quite problematic to deal with, but fortunately, there are not many. Then, next to these, there are other realities that, though they prefer the Latin Mass in the traditional liturgical form of the Council of Trent with the Paul VI missal of 1962, they do not in any way reject Vatican II. In this case, they do not place in doubt the doctrinal principles of the Council but only what concerns the liturgical discipline. This is a substantial distinction.

In the meantime, the decision taken by Francis has had negative consequences and effects. It was unexpected, and, for traditionalists, it was a slap in the face. The prohibition of using this liturgical form dug a trench, causing much pain. It would have been more useful to make a distinction between the substance of the sacraments that derive from Christ through the apostles and are essential and the liturgical forms that exist in the Church in various rites. And in the Church, there are twenty-three rites: among them, the Malabar, Chrysostom, Basilian, Ambrosian, and so on. They differ only in form. For example, before the year 1000, the Creed was not even recited in the Mass.

The prohibition imposed on the so-called traditionalists did no one any good. Acting in this way, Pope Francis seems to have given ear to a group of advisers without realizing that this provision would take on the contours of a mere demonstration of power.

Was the decision not made by the pope?

Of course it was made by him, but the influence of a close circle of advisers is undeniable — in particular, of several professors at the Athenaeum of St. Anselm, who went to the pope and conditioned him in pursuit of their own interests. I know several of them, and according to them, the only legitimate liturgical form is the conciliar one. To them, all the other forms must disappear, whereas the Council enlarged the horizons in a harmonious unity of the essential. They proved themselves to be more ideologues than theologians. Unfortunately, in this pontificate, dogmatic theology is irrelevant, as if it had little to say. Consequently, the prohibition of the celebration of the Mass according to the Tridentine Rite has prevailed over the substance of the Eucharist, to which everyone (and I repeat, everyone) should direct their gaze.

I recently had occasion to visit France, where the new bishop of a diocese prohibited the Confirmation of a group of adolescents simply because the ceremony would have been held in the Traditional Rite in Latin. I was amazed because this bishop seemed more interested in the Latin liturgy than in imparting the sacrament to these children. It's as if one favored the form over the substance.

Can you explain this distinction better?

When Benedict XVI intervened, he decided that a criterion of separation must be made between the Vatican II rite and the old Tridentine Rite, which, he said, remained legitimate though extraordinary. Naturally, he had to face fierce internal opposition despite having established the matter with the idea of fostering unity and a progressive inclusion with traditionalists. Years later, under the current pontificate, a group of Francis's advisers complained, saying that Benedict XVI had taken a false step with that measure, causing further divisions, and that, in order to recover balance, it would be better to return to the previous state of things. Thus was Francis manipulated. A short time later, *Summorum Pontificum* (the apostolic letter of Pope Benedict XVI, published in the form of a motu proprio on July 7, 2007, regarding the use of the old missal) was abrogated. Some spiteful people hold that Francis is not that interested in the liturgy, preferring other means for opening processes aimed at modernizing the Church. And when they point out to him that there is internal resistance to the reforms being carried out, he acts without making any distinction between the groups of "traditionalists." I don't know how things stand, but the consequences in terms of unity are counterproductive and are a source of useless tensions.

Can you give some details?

I am speaking of the tendency to reform the Church in a Protestant sense. I am speaking of a creeping protestantization, of a liberal vision without consideration of the tradition. Cardinal Carlo Maria Martini stated that since the time of the Enlightenment, two centuries of delay has accumulated in the Church. Much time has to be recovered to reach modernity. A line of action requires that innovations be made in order to be in step with today's world — on the family issue, for example, and also on life issues. Protestants (who were the first to undertake this process of change at the time of Luther) appear in the eyes of the world to be absolutely modern, while Catholicism is perceived as quite backward — an old, dusty institution that fails to listen to the world's evolution.

The Protestant liturgical celebration seems by now a symposium deprived of the dimension of the salvific suffering of the Cross and of the Eucharist. It is within this framework of expectations that an ideological current within this pontificate has taken hold, placing "traditionalists" among the opponents of the modernization underway, desired even by the pope. These "traditionalists" are considered responsible for the many delays of Francis's reforms. The situation should move us to reflect.

Recently in France, I celebrated Mass in the preconciliar rite in Latin. I don't feel I'm a heretic for this. Ever since the Council of Trent, it was established that, in the Church, various rites exist, although the substance remains the same. Jesus instituted the Eucharist, and this is the substance of the sacrament for Catholics.

Is the Latin Mass no longer celebrated in St. Peter's?

It was wrong to prohibit the Latin Mass according to the Paul VI missal in St. Peter's. It was an arbitrary act, besides being a pastoral imprudence. In the eyes of the world, we are prolonging internal disputes that make no sense; we cannot be arguing over these matters. What happened during the sack of Constantinople comes to mind, when the Turks besieged the city, and at the moment of greatest danger, the theologians were caught up in debating among themselves about the color of our Lady's eyes. That is approximately what is happening now. People seem blind, and in this complex situation, the task of pastors is to unite, not to divide. Rather than arguing about the liturgy, should we not be challenging those who affirm that the Church is a sort of NGO, working, above all, in the social sphere, rather than evangelizing? I wonder what the color of the chasuble or the lace on the altar cloth could possibly matter to the world. Or even if there are enough flowers on the altar. It's a question of tastes and perhaps of local traditions. The heart of the problem is another, and it's evident: the defense of the sacrament of the Eucharist. Well beyond lace!

People under pressure from secularization have a nuanced perception of this reality of faith. On Sundays, we see many people gathered in St. Peter's Square for the pope's midday blessing and to listen to the Angelus. The same people, however, almost certainly did not go to Mass. Perhaps they do not know that the Sunday precept in any parish celebrated by any priest is more important than the papal blessing, which, though very authoritative, is not a sacramental action. It's as if there is a widespread lack of balance, and thus, we must reflect on the essential. For an architect, it's more important to study the statics of a building than the color of the paint on its walls.

Cardinal Martini shed light on many delays. Wasn't he right?

What does that mean, and in relation to what? How can the Church be delayed with respect to the substance of the gospel? Irenaeus of Lyon said Christ brought in Himself all innovation; Christ is, in substance, insurmountable — although it's obvious we cannot develop a pastoral strategy as if we lived in a medieval society. We have our megacities today, societies structured differently, complex realities, and consequently, we must have different pastoral forms, presence in schools, in the workplace, in families, and in every possible setting to be closer to people. We certainly cannot say that we once spoke of God's kingdom, whereas now we have to limit ourselves to social themes. The content of revelation remains Christ, who per se cannot be "delayed." Human thought is reflected in modern sciences and in human evolution and is to be blended with the doctrine of the apostles. Theological reflection must respond to developments in science, but only to offer the content of revelation and redemption. After all, the astronaut of today is the same human being who lived in Sicily two thousand years before Christ, in the time of Magna Graecia. He has need of the very same friendship with God, although his living conditions are quite different. The task of theology is to make a synthesis of society's ongoing progress.

You seem to suggest that Pope Francis "detests" theologians, as if he had an aversion toward them. Are you not going too far?

I would say that the question can be inserted into a framework of events. Francis has stated a number of times that he is on the side of simple people, embracing their pain, their daily hardships and joys. But then he seems not to show accord with theologians who, in his opinion, put themselves at times between the people, just like Jesus with the doctors of the law. Once he even said that if there were no theologians, there would not have been so many divisions and ruptures among Christians. Both the Great Schism[6] and the Protestant Reformation remain concentrations of complex problems — Luther's position, justification by faith, the question of the Filioque, and so on. These are theories that only those who study theology can understand

---

[6] It becomes clear from what follows that Cardinal Müller means the Great Schism of 1054 and not the Western Schism (1378–1417), as in the Italian text.

completely. Theology is necessary for explaining Christianity in a world that is changing rapidly. We are not living in the time of the ancient Romans. St. Augustine reacted to the collapse of the Roman Empire by writing his *De Civitate Dei*, explaining that the Church was not dependent on the protection of the Roman Empire, long since Christianized. Today the political situation is different, and one must apply the substance of his *De Civitate Dei* to other systems of power: Putin, Biden, or Xi. The challenge is how Christianity will be able to continue to help humanity. Faith in Christ does not depend on the elaboration of the thought of a tight circle of intellectuals. Children can believe too. Theologians are called to clarify and defend the Faith. In the First Letter of St. Peter 3:15, it says to give answers to everyone, on condition that faith and reason are united. And faith is not only an emotional act, irrational or intuitive; it is knowledge that captures the light coming from God.

Staying in the theological sphere, a few years ago, the text of the Our Father was changed in Italian. The phrase "lead us not into temptation" was replaced with "do not abandon us to temptation."

It seems to me an incomprehensible modification. "Lead us not into temptation" are the words of Jesus in the New Testament. In theory, that text cannot be changed nor the Greek version perfected. It's the case of an incorrect translation, although at times it's complicated to translate well and to try to improve on the words of Jesus. We can explain or interpret misunderstandings, but we certainly cannot alter the original sense. "Lead us not into temptation": in the Bible, we have Satan, who accompanies us into temptation, and it remains a trial that God allows to test us, to examine us. Being oriented toward sin is an innate impulse in man. Whoever modified the prayer was certainly animated by good intentions, but the outcome does not reflect what is indicated in the original text. Fortunately, the Our Father was changed only in Italian and not in other languages. In German, for example, it remained unaltered.

But if that's the way things are, why did none of the pope's collaborators warn him in time about this error in the translation of the Our Father in Italian?

I think my successor, Cardinal Ladaria, did so, and I know other people did too, but theologians as a category in this historical predicament have little opportunity. They are, as I said, kept on the margins. The phrase "The Word was made flesh" comes to mind. The Greek word for *flesh*, *sarx*, has a wide significance that begs classification. All such technical terms cannot be changed.

What has produced the change in the Our Father? Unfortunately, another rift, one of many, with a backdrop of desperation. Yes, of desperation, because the common people who grew up with this invocation in the family and in the parish are disoriented. And to this is added the *vulnus* [wound] caused by the galaxy of the so-called traditionalists, who, as I explained before, include those as well who accept Vatican II. The final effect is the same. All those, without distinction, who protest or raise criticisms or experience legitimate perplexities are branded as the great enemies of the pope, the bad guys, the disobedient who should be punished. But this reading is oversimplified.

Many statistical analyses indicate that the Church in Europe is in a waning phase, to the contrary of the Muslim minority, which is showing a surprising vitality. How do you explain this?

In democratic and developed societies, there is freedom and the right to decide which religion to belong to, and we can never place in doubt the right of each person to freedom of conscience. Nevertheless, the Church, having received from God her mandate to go into the world and preach the gospel, is not comparable to a state. All the baptized are disciples of Christ. Muslims have, on the other hand, a different plan of action: essentially, they want to subject humanity to their faith and carry this out with more aggressive methods. For us Christians, the Faith is never a submission; it's a free response.

During the pontificate of John Paul II, an important document was approved and signed by then-Cardinal Joseph Ratzinger, **Dominus Iesus,** *in which the superiority of Christianity with respect to other faiths was reaffirmed. Do you think that the Catholic Church has renounced evangelizing unbelievers or people of other faiths in Europe and in the world?*

Christianity is personal adhesion to the gospel. The pastoral practice that we carry out does not foresee the necessity of convincing those who do not believe in Christ. The transmission of the Faith remains a commitment, however, and that means witnessing to Christian culture and living one's personal adhesion to God in a total and coherent manner. We all must be witnesses to universal salvation, not only the pope and the cardinals or bishops but every individual believer. We cannot promote an aggressive Christianization or force people or even persuade them with deception. A free, personal conviction of conversion to Jesus Christ is needed. Consequently, preaching to Muslims or to people of other religions, bringing them to receive Baptism, after an autonomous, personal maturation, is a long process.

The Church in Europe is visibly weary. She seems no longer to believe in herself, and at times, even her representatives are no longer so convinced of the truth of Christianity. It's paradoxical. They live as if all religions are, in the end, the same, nearly interchangeable. And it's well known that the frame of reference has to do with currents of agnosticism and a creeping relativism: everyone believes in his or her own truth without focusing on the inheritance of faith Christ left us, forgetting that Christianity remains a fundamental factor for a society orientated toward living peacefully, fraternally, and justly. Other Christians, influenced by Kant, reduce religion to ethics. They maintain that Christianity is only one of humanity's faiths, and thus they reduce it to immanent culture, for which transcendence is transformed into a vague higher conviction: one God is the same as another God.

There are those who affirm that the Christian religion is functional for the peaceful coexistence of humanity, and in this way, religion becomes humanism. It seems as if it's sufficient to help the needy, to avoid waging war, and to be charitable; but to be a Christian, that is not enough because we have to believe in Jesus Christ, the Son of God, the Messiah, who became flesh, died, and rose for humanity and is the only one in whom our hope lies. How can those who do not believe in the Resurrection call themselves Christians? In the Acts of the Apostles, it says that Christians are those who believe in Jesus — an incarnated God for whom one accepts the consequences of life: "In Antioch the disciples were for the first time called Christians" (Acts 11:26).

Today however, we can observe a divided Christianity. One insists much on love of neighbor, one's brother or sister, but at its origin is God's love, the God whom one must love with one's whole heart. Otherwise, the Faith is a tree without roots. One may not exclude from the horizontal dimension of the truth — namely, love of one's neighbor — the vertical dimension — namely, the transcendent. These two aspects must not be confused or one privileged to the detriment of the other. The Cross is also harmony.

As for *Dominus Iesus*, it's a magisterial document of the highest value, despite not being very fashionable. And this is the problem of the Church today. Christ, as sole Mediator between God and man, remains a challenge for unbelievers. If the Christians of the first centuries, under the Roman Empire, had stopped at charitable works, they would not have been persecuted. The problem was that they believed in God and in Jesus and not in the emperor as a divinity, and thus they were sent to die. It's cause for reflection today that some bishops prefer not to affirm publicly that Christ is the only God so as not to be criticized by media and to avoid positions that might sound nonconformist or politically incorrect. And perhaps not by chance, the majority of mass media in the West end up being riddled by secular currents that weaken the Church and aim at de-Christianizing society. And yet the Catholic Church, notwithstanding her intrinsic weakness, continues to represent a bulwark against the massification of thought. Christ teaches us to be free. *Dominus Iesus* expresses what, for Christians, is the absolute truth.

But does the Church not risk being divisive in this way?

God is one in monotheism: Allah, Yahweh, Christ. There exists only one God for the Jewish, Muslim, and Christian faiths. Greek Aristotelian philosophy also spoke of one God. Christianity and Judaism have their roots in the Old Testament, while Muhammad constructed an image of God that is anti-Christian. He affirmed that the Trinity was a false interpretation, although, for Islam, there is a trinitarian relationship, albeit founded in Allah, his son, and Mary. For Muslims, the concept of God centers essentially on power. Furthermore, they are deprived of the sacraments. The Quran speaks of a merciful God and might recall the words contained in the Old Testament, but it does not seem to be coherent with the idea of mercy that Muslims imagine, considering the militant activity against non-Muslims. It is no coincidence that in the countries where Islam dominates (or dominated), Christians suffer persecution and certainly do not have it easy.

We read the news from around the world. The situation is critical in Nigeria, in Indonesia, and even in the Emirates and Iran. In Pakistan, Christians are accused of blasphemy and end up in prison for this. The case of Asia Bibi is emblematic: a woman condemned to death for blasphemy and then released after a widespread international campaign. Every year, Amnesty International compiles a long list highlighting the ongoing persecutions, and we do well to consult it. The document on universal brotherhood, signed by Pope Francis in the Arab Emirates in 2019 to draw Islam and Christianity nearer, surely originated with good intentions. It remains, however, a document for the elite in Islamic academic circles. Only with great difficulty will it be able to penetrate the mass of faithful Muslims.

Do you fear that Europe, as a political construct, might fail, seeing that, at its foundations, it seems to lack entirely a spiritual or cultural bond?

In effect, with this creeping nihilism, I think it risks not surviving much longer. I say this with regret and grief, but a union cannot be constructed exclusively on a monetary foundation, without Christianity as a historical cultural element, with only political and economic instruments. Europe seems to mirror the image projected every year by Davos, where seated around the same table are only politicians, capitalists, and philanthropists intent on saving the world, constructing a new planet on the basis of money, which inevitably takes the upper hand over appeals to other values. It's absurd, but that's how it is.

Matteo Salvini, Viktor Orbán, Donald Trump, and Giorgia Meloni are examples of politicians who have not earned much sympathy in the Vatican for their opposition to the arrival of immigrants. But then these politicians blatantly exhibit rosaries at rallies and say they are in favor of the traditional family. Is this not an incoherent position for a believer?

Perhaps one ought to move beyond simple thinking and confront complex questions such as immigration with a different, more articulated approach. Immigration is not a subject for dynamics like the clashes between Guelphs and Ghibellines, and consequently, there are many variables to take into consideration: the demographic effects, impacts on social cohesion, the lack of common policy, the risks of creating unmanageable ghettos with repercussions on security. It is not at all easy for those who govern. It is clear that politicians — Salvini as well as others — retain that the demographic catastrophe cannot be resolved in Europe by opening the borders indiscriminately, without rules, to tens of millions of Africans. Moreover, history teaches us that solutions of this sort cannot function. It's said we should work toward a true integration, but this is a process to be realized gradually, by means of creating guaranteed corridors and certainly a more equitable distribution in Europe. The weight of the arrivals must not fall only upon the nations that lie on the Mediterranean: Greece, Cyprus, Italy, Spain, Malta, and France.

What will the Church in Europe be like in fifty years?

No one can know this for certain. It will probably be a minority; at any rate, we are already there. Now we are 18 percent of the world's population. There will eventually be a foreseeable decline, above all in the Old World. Unfortunately, there is not at present an intense missionary activity in Europe to witness the gospel to Muslims and migrants arriving. But the Church will not die. The Roman emperor Diocletian wanted to destroy it completely. He gave orders to burn all the documents to demolish the memory of it, but it served no purpose. Also in Germany, after the Lutheran reform, the Catholic Church had nearly disappeared, until the Jesuits and Capuchins took over and Catholicism found new vigor and recovered many territories.

Has not the moment arrived perhaps for a Vatican III, as the deceased German cardinal Karl Lehmann affirmed back in the beginning of the millennium?

An eventual Vatican Council III would have to be placed in continuum with Vatican II and Vatican I, naturally encouraging reflection toward favoring a Church more open to the laity. The rendering of the Council a myth that followed in the years immediately after the Council, from the sixties on, understood this event as a compromise between the papacy and the bishops, in a synthesis of faith and unity that helped us move forward, connecting the Church with the world. Perhaps the next council could confront transhumanism or concentrate on how to bring about the triumph of the dignity of man in reference to a world by now under total technical, economical, and political control. In my opinion, the great question that should be asked is where human dignity fits in today. What perception does one have of this? One ought not to speak so much of the Church as a self-referential subject. We cannot reflect infinitely upon ourselves. We need to lift our gaze, fly far, widen the horizons. If a child is hungry and we are discussing maternity, perhaps it is necessary to direct our attention to the child as well. We ought to develop the powerful message of Christ for humanity, and instead, the Church has the tendency to talk about herself, to concentrate on herself. We have a Dicastery for Evangelization precisely for thinking big, but then we always end up reducing the evangelization of the Church to a dicastery.

Germany

In Germany, a synodal revision was initiated with revolutionary traits. Unanimous requests are emerging for enormous changes. I'm thinking of celibacy, women's Ordination, the blessing of gay couples. Where is the German Church heading?

In Germany, the word *synodality* is used to camouflage something quite different. Indeed, it sounds good: *synodal* refers to walking together. But forward movement in Christianity should be Christ, the Incarnate Word of God. It is neither possible nor imaginable to modify the doctrine of the apostles to one's own liking, almost as if it were a political platform, as many German Catholics would like to do. It is not an electoral system with candidates or parties that agitate to bring in the vote of the electors. We believers can be witnesses to the revelation of God but not to manipulators. The bishops or the pope cannot be subjected to democratic mechanisms such as voting on the part of the Church, as many are requesting in Germany.

The dogmatic constitution *Dei Verbum* (no. 10) states that the Word of God is present by means of the Bible and the apostolic tradition of the Church, for which the Magisterium is the source neither of revelation nor of the truth; rather, it insists that the Word of God be respected. In brief, we are listeners and do not dictate to God what He must reveal about Himself. At times, I think there are too many bishops in circulation who are not up to the task and who do not know Catholic hermeneutics well, seeing that they cultivate the analytical narrative of the Second Vatican Council, on the basis of which the doctrine of the Church could be changed according to the preferences of the people. This is not true. And we do well to clarify another point — namely, that all of this does not conform to the Catholic Faith. It must be said.

Is this why one speaks of the democratization of the Church?

The word is abused, although we are all obviously in favor of democracy. Nevertheless, the essence of the Church cannot be subjected to any form of politicization. We can promote associations, but the Church remains the People of God, and God is the subject, and Christ is the Head of His Body. The Holy Spirit is the one who fills His temple. This means that the Church, with her hierarchy, is not a form of government, and the bishops and priests are the personal representatives of Christ and not of the people. Jesus Christ certainly did not give His apostles spiritual power to govern in a monarchy or in a form of autocracy.

What important requests is the synodal way in Germany making?

The concept of Church that is emerging has nothing to do with Catholic theology. The Church is not an association parallel to the state, of an economic or private nature, and it cannot be naturalized as if it were a worldly structure. It's emblematic that in the documents published in Germany, the word *God* almost never appears. Instead, a worldly, political vision emerges, as if the Church were a purely human organization, subjected to the changes of men, to be developed on the basis of their wishes. In the Church, however, the power of men over other men does not exist: the Church is something quite different, and the ecclesiastical authority does not allow the reigning pontiff to impose his personal will. The pope is the visible head of unity, not a monarch: he governs in another sense, as a pastor, not like a prime minister. Moreover, the pope is not an expression of a lobby or of associations. In the Gospel of Matthew, chapter 20, Jesus says that the powerful of this world govern men according to their interests, "but among you it must not be that way" (see v. 26). The only shepherd is Christ.

If these are the presuppositions, it seems nearly a given that a full-blown schism is maturing in Germany.

I think a situation much worse than schism might be taking shape: we are witnessing a separation of the local churches from the center in Rome; they are practically abandoning sacramentality. This is apostasy, therefore, and not schism. It is worse because it means concretely abandoning the foundations of Christianity. It is a Church without God, without revelation. But what is the Church without Christ or without revelation? A nearly civil organization. In a gathering of the Katholikentag, the German bishops pushed all the way to giving Communion to some Muslims present and not only to Protestants. Whoever distributed the consecrated Hosts surely must have been convinced, deep down, that those people were good and respectable, and they probably were; but with that gesture, the meaning of the Eucharist was changed. As if you could receive the Body of Christ without having faith. A bishop from Stuttgart changed the liturgy, mutating the substance of the Faith. It's as if there were a plan to develop a flexible, ecumenical liturgy, open to all religions and even to atheists. When the founding principles of the Church collapse, or the sacraments are distorted, complete chaos descends, and every novelty is licit. As a result, the entire edifice is brought to collapse.

You are speaking about a sinister, unimaginable scenario.

Certainly, the risk is the end of Christianity in Germany: Communion without belief in Christ means the twilight of the German Church. Protestants can already receive the Host, even though they officially deny Catholic doctrine. In Germany, the president of the Protestant council has stated that it suffices to repeat the words of Christ and then everyone can believe in whatever he or she wants. The Church, however, has a different position: no one can belong to the Church while denying the Faith.

Fortunately, not all agree with this situation. During this long synodal way, there have been German cardinals who have manifested strong criticism of this path. Theologians such as Cardinals Kasper, Woelki, Cordes, and Brandmüller come to mind. One of the requests that emerges with great insistence in the debates concerns the abolition of celibacy. Naturally, this can be discussed, given that it is a matter of a consolidated tradition of the Church and because it is not a necessary requirement for the priesthood. There are married clergy, in fact, even in the Latin Church. What can never be placed in discussion, however, is the Real Presence of Christ in the Eucharist. The Son of God is really present in the consecrated Host and can never be distributed in an indiscriminate way to those who do not believe, Muslims or atheists. This would be sacrilege.

What is the point of this undertaking that began with the approval of Rome?

I repeat, and I'm convinced: this will lead to the destruction of the Catholic Church in Germany. Certain requests shake the foundations to the point of reverberating elsewhere too. What's happening to the Church in Barcelona comes to mind; there, they are already talking about the reform, and they are concentrating on women's priesthood and the blessing of homosexual couples. In this case as well, the synodal agenda proposed by some groups never mentions evangelization, how to preach the gospel, or how to transmit faith in Jesus Christ. The Church is present as a social organization dedicated to refugees and the poor — certainly important aspects, but forgetting along the way that the Church's mission is the sacrament of eternal salvation in communion with God. For us Christians, the meaning of our being on earth is that of having a divine vocation.

In Germany, there are bishops who have begun to give blessings to homosexual couples, recognizing homosexual love, despite Rome's prohibitions. Naturally, this strong tendency is opposed in the Vatican. Through a **Responsum** *of the Congregation for the Doctrine of the Faith, it was established that it was an illicit act, not permitted by the liturgy. But there are homosexual [unions of] Catholic couples that last over thirty years, demonstrating dedication, care, and reciprocal love and offer a visible model of affectivity. Do you think that the development of theological thought in the future might admit forms of consecration in order not to emphasize the existence of an A-series love and a B-series love? Should love not always be considered the same?*

The problem emerged because of a mentality less and less in line with doctrine, influenced by the effects of gender ideology, which promotes a concept of human sexuality light-years away from Christian anthropology. In recent decades, sociological and political pressures of a certain importance have been added to this mentality, not the least of these pressures coming from the European Union, for which the right to abortion and the rights of "rainbow" families are among its community values. Whoever dares to doubt this tendency gets silenced for being medieval, obscurantist, illiberal. In Germany now, you can decide to change your name and sex with great ease. There is a deputy in the Bundestag who declared he had become a woman. I was struck by a headline about an Englishman condemned for aggravated sexual violence. Once in prison, he announced that, in reality, he had a woman's nature, and so the prison wardens, in order to guarantee his new identity, transferred him to a women's penitentiary, where, unfortunately, he raped several female inmates in their cells.

The Church should create a pastoral path for homosexual couples, to avoid damaging in any way the concept of union between a man and a woman, a reality derived from creation and mirrored in the gospel. Sacramental marriage admits only couples of opposite sexes, formed by one male and one female. All other forms are excluded from the blessing because parish priests and bishops receive the power to bless directly from God at the moment of their consecration. The contrary would be sacrilegious. We read in the book of Genesis that Adam and Eve were blessed, from the Latin *bene dicere*, because they guaranteed the continuation of the human species. The blessings given by certain pastors to gay couples in Germany (and elsewhere too) have no sacred value whatsoever. I have friends, men and women, who live their homosexuality without demanding any blessing. It is possible, however, to work on a pastoral approach to guide these people on the path of Jesus Christ. Many pastoral forms are elaborated — for youth, for the elderly, for businessmen, for prisoners, and so forth — and it would be natural to develop specific ways for welcoming homosexual couples, loved by God as others, without envisaging the blessing.

Forgive me if I insist, but isn't there a way to find a formula to recognize the goodness of their love, keeping the sacramental path distinct from the pastoral one? After all, it is love.

I agree that love is a good thing, love will save the world, but we cannot accept the love between two men or two women who have sexual relations against nature. This is not the love inscribed in Genesis; it is a personal relationship, profound, but certainly something else. Even so, sexuality can be contextualized only if a conjugal design exists. The fact is that homosexuals do not have the right to have intimate relations, as explained in the *Catechism*.

In Germany, however, the request to modify the Catechism is growing from below — particularly the part that treats homosexuality, especially where relations are prohibited to Catholic homosexuals. The only road identified for them is chastity, a path that seems so cruel and discriminatory.

The prevalent, centuries-old logic leads people to sustain the liceity of having blessings for gay couples. The *Catechism of the Catholic Church* explains the question in an exhaustive way from the moral point of view, just like some equally clear documents from the Congregation for the Doctrine of the Faith. Pope Francis recently expressed disapproval of the blessings, authorizing a *Responsum*, although he has not yet wanted to express himself openly. In the Curia, one says with a certain malice that the pontiff positions himself according to the last visitor he has received at Santa Marta, but these are only nasty rumors. With the American Jesuit Fr. James Martin, for example, the pope happened to pronounce in favor of these pastoral forms; then, receiving in audience more traditionalist people contrary to the blessings, he manifested other convictions. In any case, it is not simple to proclaim the honest Word of God, going against the current with respect to the mainstream. It's much more comfortable to please public opinion and to flatter the worldly logic. And it is also due to this substantial silence on the part of the pope that today there are so many who do not fully understand the foundation of indissolubility of Catholic marriage. Clarity is lacking. It is not so much inventiveness of a historical construction but, rather, an element derived from the Divine Word, from revelation. Pagans, in fact, did not have the concept of monogamy; it was Christ who changed the direction of history. St. John the Baptist repeats to Herod that it is not lawful to take his brother's wife (Matt. 14:3–4). We know how this story ended — with the decapitation of the Baptist.

After the Synod on the Family, many of the faithful asked the pope for explanations about the numerous doctrinal doubts raised by the exhortation Amoris Laetitia *regarding the concessions to divorced and remarried Catholics. How was this matter resolved?*

It wasn't resolved at all, and the doubts are all still there, in full view. No one has ever responded in all these years. The fact is that sacramental marriage cannot be reduced to living with another person; it remains a definitive decision in the framework of the relationship of Christ the Bridegroom with His Spouse, the Church. Christ obviously comes before all else. The Word of the Lord on this matter is clear: "What therefore God has joined together, let not man put asunder" (Mark 10:9). Unfortunately, the Christian religion has been condensed into a complex of values, ideas, or social activities, while losing along the way that which was essential and basic to the experience of faith — namely, the encounter with Christ and the total renewal of man in an eschatological perspective. Christian Matrimony is a sacrament, and therefore it is the will of God that marriage be the intimate and unique union between one man and one woman only. This union is the spring from which flows the family. In a basically individualistic world, marriage is no longer perceived as an offering capable of leading a human being to fullness by participating in love. In our secularized environments, indissolubility is among the most incomprehensible things to be accepted.

It was Msgr. Giacomo Morandi who signed the **Responsum,** *which contained the absolute prohibition of blessing gay couples. At the time, he was secretary of the Congregation for the Doctrine of the Faith, and he is now bishop in Reggio Emilia [in northern Italy]. It is said that he was moved by Pope Francis very quickly from Rome to Emilia precisely because of this document, which, after its publication, raised a strong wave of protest from the more reformist wing of the Church. Was that really the case?*

I have been out of the Congregation for years, and I wouldn't be able to give details. The pope's decisions are often difficult to understand fully. It is true that Morandi's transfer was spoken of as due to the *Responsum,* but that's only speculation, and no one is capable of reconstructing the matter from its origins. When he was called to Rome, Bishop Morandi was surely counted among the great friends of the pontiff; he was in his graces. Then, over the years, he must have fallen into disgrace a bit, a frequent dynamic in Santa Marta. In any case, his transfer to Reggio Emilia cannot be read only as a punishment. Being a diocesan bishop, he can dedicate himself to the faithful, show a pastoral heart, and embrace the life of the Church in the concrete territorial reality, and this is beautiful. Leaving the Diocese of Regensburg, when I was called by Benedict XVI, was an enormous sacrifice for me. I left behind me a territory of 1,300,000 Catholics to go and concern myself with safeguarding the doctrine of the Faith. Let's be clear: this was a challenge and a stimulating path. I was made a cardinal, I enjoyed fulfillment, but what it's like to guide the flock, to share hopes and problems, to resolve dramas, to find solutions, to teach youth, to console those in broken marriages, and to accompany the dying has no equal. This remains the heart of pastoral service.

If, from the theological point of view, there is no hope of modifying the **Catechism** *regarding homosexuality, giving the possibility to two*

Catholic men or two Catholic women who love each other to live their sexuality without moral condemnation from the Church, what can be done?

Some things can be reconsidered, but on this point, the profession of faith cannot be modified. The *Catechism* is no longer taught in the version drafted by the Council of Trent. The methodology has changed, but its structure has remained the same; the Ten Commandments are intact. The pope, for example, intervened on the death penalty, affirming that, in the past, it was acceptable in specific circumstances, whereas today there is the conviction that there are too many innocent people condemned in the world in dictatorial nations. The modification was possible because it was not a matter of divine revelation. If it's a matter of social doctrine, theology can contemplate a different path, adapting to the changes in the general situation and in the superior intention to adapt moral principles. In the Middle Ages, for example, there was no industrialization, and in the time of Innocent III, one could not have imagined condemning the use of the atomic bomb. At the Council of Trent, they never discussed organ transplants, which were still an unknown procedure.

So it is clear that we cannot modify the *Catechism* on the question of homosexuality because it directly concerns revealed doctrine. St. Paul and the four evangelists spoke about it, transmitting one sole version — that marriage is between a man and a woman, exactly as Jesus intended:

> Have you not read that he who made them from the beginning made them male and female, and said, "For this reason a man shall leave his father and mother and be joined to his wife, and the two shall become one"? So they are no longer two but one. What therefore God has joined together, let not man put asunder. (Matt. 19:4–6)

The *Catechism*, then, expresses the revealed doctrine and cannot be subjected to the winds of fashion. This will mean we will have to resist negative public opinion.

At times, it comes to mind how, in Russia, state atheism dominated and the Church was persecuted for eighty years because it was judged anti-modern. But the Church survived. In the Greco-Roman world as well, public opinion and intellectuals at the time were against Christians. Well, patience if we are countercultural! Origen started a bitter polemic with a philosopher, Celsus, from the Neoplatonic school, precisely on the concept of God. Celsus said that the God of the Christians had to be false because he held the Incarnation and the Resurrection to be impossible. With these elements, the debate protracted until the time of Julian the Apostate. Then there were the apologists such as Justin, who defended Christianity and its doctrine. In the end, Christians are used to holding the line and not allowing themselves to be influenced by fashions or to bend under pressure. St. Paul writes to the Corinthians about the wisdom of the world against the foolishness of God:

> For Jews demand signs and Greeks seek wisdom, but we preach Christ crucified, a stumbling block to Jews and folly to Gentiles, but to those who are called, both Jews and Greeks, Christ the power of God and the wisdom of God. For the foolishness of God is wiser than men, and the weakness of God is stronger than men. (1 Cor. 1:22–25)

Christianity is the religion of contrasts, and Christians have experience with facing a de-Christianized culture. Today, however, two hundred years after the Enlightenment, this clash is evident, and we are sliding down a slope. The great politicians of the European Union aim more or less consciously at the de-Christianization of our thought, at weakening Christian roots even on the cultural level.

They would like to leave Christianity to believers, to relegate it to a sort of civil religion containing only some elements of spirituality, and they reject Christianity as a critical, prophetic, alternative solution. They would like to domesticate the gospel too. The danger is in the advance of a new form of absolutism that contemplates man as a mere material reality with his pleasures and desires within a nearly anesthetized mass.

We can set sexuality in this framework as well — no longer considered as a great gift of God. Responsibility for spouse and children and the sequence of generations to come no longer assumes a central role. Sexuality, on the other hand, becomes an act aimed exclusively at one's own subjective pleasure, a sort of drug for calming a nihilistic horizon, where everything, in the end, appears nearly empty of meaning. As described by Sartre's school of existentialism, there is no room for a common meaning, for a Logos, because the Cosmos seems to have disappeared. Everything is chance, and man has no meaning for himself, and so nothing is the fruit of the Creator's will. You are no longer willed by the Creator, who loves you as a being, but are rather the product of the combination and evolution of elements. Mere materialism, what Epicurus and Democritus expounded in their works, nothing more. And in this frame of reference, discipline and being subject to limits go against the logic. Better to live following one's desires, one's pleasures, and so when illness and old age arrive, even suicide becomes a right and euthanasia easily procured. Christians cannot accept this deviation precisely because they believe in God and in the absolute value of the person. They do not have the right to destroy themselves because life is a gift from the Lord. Suicide cannot be merely a personal act because it implies responsibility toward the Creator and toward loved ones. The Church does not formulate condemnations of suicides, but the Christian vision does not contemplate the right to take one's life.

In Germany, there's a Catholic movement that would like to write the word God *with an asterisk to make it more inclusive of various existing diversities. A step forward?*

Blasphemy: God created them male and female, and consequently, to affirm that the Creator is a combination of two sexes or of many biological sexes and to make of it a creature of our imagination makes no sense. Greek mythology had divinities that were projections of creation, they were presented as hybrid figures, but the Bible applies a clear distinction between Creator and creature. For this reason, God has no sex and cannot be a combination of the two sexes. God has no body; God is spirit and truth. In relationship to us, God is Father. Jesus spoke of the Father to express the relationships within the mystery of the Trinity. God is not a parent, a father as we understand in a biological sense. He cannot be one because He has no biological sex. In the same way, God is not a mother. Mary is the Mother of God because from her was born Jesus with His human nature.

During his brief reign, John Paul I spoke of God as mother, but only in a metaphorical sense. In Germany, certain ideas are affirmed because fewer and fewer people believe in God. Those who promote the project of wanting to write *God* with an asterisk are only projecting sociological models; they no longer have knowledge of the biblical God. One can say that God is loving and maternal, as a mother can be, but not God-mother in a biological sense. In the same way, God is not our father in a biological sense. Every page in the Bible states that the God of Israel is not like the gods of the pagans. What is happening in the West represents a paganization of Christianity. This is exactly what Feuerbach asserted regarding God — that He was a product of our imagination.

No Popes Emeriti

On February 11, 2013, Pope Benedict XVI announced to the world his resignation7 — a gesture that would revolutionize the papacy and create inevitable problems as well for the cohabitation in the Vatican of two pontiffs, one reigning and the other emeritus. Do you remember that day?

The news of his resignation surprised me as well. I did not expect it. It was the Swiss cardinal Kurt Koch, whom I had met that day by chance, who told me the pope was going to step down soon. I had just returned from a long business trip to the United States, with fifteen hours of flying in me. I had just landed and had missed the meeting of the consistory for the creation of new saints. I was stunned by the announcement; I couldn't believe it. I couldn't believe it. The pope had confided in very few people, and I was not one of them, and to be honest, I was hurt.

It was obvious that, formally, he could resign,[8] but it was equally clear that the real problem to resolve concerned (and still concerns

---

[7] The Italian *dimesso* and *dimissioni* correspond usually to *resigned* and *resignation*. The delicacy and difficulty of assigning a term to this unique circumstance has prompted me to indicate in footnotes the precise term used each time.

[8] Here the term is *rinunciare,* "renounce."

today) the consequences of this choice. After a bishop retires,[9] he remains in the College; the pope, however, cannot be considered just any bishop. Being the bishop of Rome and the Successor of Peter — the visible and permanent principle of unity in the Church — his figure poses questions for the most part unresolved, with serious consequences and matters to be clarified. Today we have a pope emeritus as well as a reigning pope in the Vatican.[10] The situation as perceived abroad by the common man is that there are two popes, each having his own sphere of influence. But this cannot be the case, precisely due to the character of the Petrine *ministerium*. The principle of unity can be realized in one person alone. Despite the terminological distinction introduced in the past few years, however, the perceived reality remains the same.

We can analyze the situation that has come about. Although the resignation[11] was formulated in the correct manner from a canonical point of view, identity dilemmas, introduced by the presence of the pope emeritus, have emerged over time. It is difficult to ignore the many people throughout the world who identify more with Benedict XVI, with his theology and his papacy (even if he resigned[12] and no longer governs), than with Francis, without a doubt a very different pontiff in style and personality. And it is precisely this uncodified dualism that has fed the disorientation. The resignation[13] introduced a crack in the Petrine principle of unity of the faith and of communion of the Church that has no equal in history and has not yet been elaborated dogmatically. The norms of canon law are insufficient. The concrete coexistence is difficult to manage for various reasons. The questions

---

[9] Here, *rinuncia*, "renounces."

[10] Written before the death of Benedict XVI on December 31, 2022.

[11] Here, *rinuncia*, "renunciation."

[12] Here, *dimesso*, "resigned."

[13] Here, *dimissioni*, "resignation."

will be doubtless confronted sooner or later because the open *vulnus* could generate unforeseen consequences in the future.

Consider what might happen if there were other popes emeriti, given that we're moving toward an age in which the average lifespan continues to increase. The *Code of Canon Law* provides for the possibility of freely abdicating,[14] given there is no duress. Does abdication[15] mean, therefore, going into retirement? In this case, is not the risk for the Church to transform the figure of the pope, to equate him, if not to reduce him, to a state functionary? St. Peter would never have imagined retiring, not in the least. Peter and Paul died martyrs. The *Code*, therefore, speaks of abdication[16] only in extreme circumstances. We might suppose severe or degenerative illnesses. We know that Pius XII had foreseen his resignation[17] and had signed a letter, in the case he was captured by Hitler during the war. But the papacy, per se, is witness even in personal suffering, following the example of Christ, who suffered on the Cross, contemplating divine grace. The figure of the Successor of Peter can be associated with an elderly, fragile man, perhaps in a wheelchair, on a mobile lift, like John Paul II. The pope cannot be enclosed simply in the cliché of the superman pontiff, resplendent, vigorous, perennially in movement. Like all men, with age, he encounters physical vicissitudes, pathologies at times incapacitating. The pontiff must also be an exterior example to offer to the world.

In essence, it's not enough to have a detailed rule to establish what should happen with resigning[18] pontiffs, perhaps a text containing clear

---

[14] Here, *rinunciare*, "renounce."
[15] Here, *rinuncia*, "renunciation."
[16] Here, *rinuncia*, "renunciation."
[17] Here, *dimissioni*, "resignation."
[18] Here, *dimissionari*, "resigning."

directives at least on concrete aspects: for example, how to dress, where to live, what type of prerogatives to be guaranteed?

In my opinion, rules cannot be made regarding resignation,[19] especially because the pope is always free and can modify the rules how and when he wills. I insist on saying that the *vulnus* that has been opened depends not so much on ecclesial law as on divine law. The essence of the Petrine service is to offer witness to Christ, in every season of life, except in cases of degenerate mental illness. It is not a matter of service like that of a minister or a functionary of the government.

In a society in which there is no longer room for the elderly, for physical decay, illness, or fragility, a pope with cancer or ALS offers witness to others who are sick and transmits hope, love, and compassion. He helps them not to lose trust, encouraging them to believe in life after death, according to the teaching of our Lord. What is already happening in the Church, imagining in the future other popes in retirement, is only an attempt to copy the dynamics at work in civil society. Naturally, I respect the personal decision of Ratzinger, made in good conscience, in freedom. I cannot, however, be silent about the ecclesiological problems that emerge from this decision, particularly regarding the coexistence of two pontiffs.

In some ways, the two protagonists have become, even against their wills, a point of attraction for Catholics with different spiritual and theological orientations or those who simply have human sympathy for one or the other. At the worst, they have become figures of identification for fringes or factions in conflict. And thus, the service of the pope to the unity of the Church ends up transforming into the exact contrary. It is obvious that, for the current pontiff, it is not so simple to carry out his ministry with the presence in the Vatican of a person who is no longer pope but who was once and who lives about three

---

[19] Here, *dimissioni,* "resignation."

hundred yards away. Fortunately, good personal relations were established between the two pontiffs through familiarity and collaboration. Nevertheless, the external exigencies do not appear easy.

Similar problems appear in dioceses as well when a bishop, having reached seventy-five years of age, retires and becomes emeritus. At that moment arises the dilemma of how to manage his presence: Where should he live? Should he stay in the city or be transferred elsewhere? Above all, will this hinder the activity of the newly appointed bishop?

As far as you know, what were the real motives that drove Benedict XVI to resign?[20] What was so grave and severe that led him to take such a step, a break with the past, to the point of abandoning the role of Successor of Peter?

He never spoke of this with me, either before the announcement or after. There is much speculation over this move. I think in that period he already felt very ill and near death. He noticed a decrease in his energy, and he had long been weakened by a violent media campaign against him — not so much due to the scandals tied with Vatileaks but, rather, over the case of the Lefebvrian bishop Williamson, a declared Holocaust denier. Williamson theorized that the Shoah had caused "only" three hundred thousand deaths. It was a hard blow for Benedict XVI, who had patiently worked to overcome the Lefebvrian schism. Animated by the best intentions, he was mending the torn unity, but the result was horrible. I remember how, in Germany, Ratzinger was accused by the press of being close to National Socialism and of having fed Hitler sympathy — he who was raised in an anti-Hitlerian, Catholic family with a disabled cousin who was eliminated by the Nazis simply because he was imperfect, suppressed according to the laws of the Third Reich, which wanted pure and perfect

---

[20] Here, *dimettersi*, "resign."

Aryans. They wrote that Ratzinger had taken part in the Hitlerjugend, knowing that everyone in his generation, from children to adolescents, could not be exempted from scholastic programs that required the brown Nazi uniforms. A bit like what happened in Italy with the Balilla. Benedict XVI was pained and, I can testify, was sorely tested.

Ratzinger could have resigned[21] then under the weight of Vatileaks, the scandal regarding his majordomo Paoletto, who stole papers from the papal apartment and made them available to the media to be published. There was a trial as well, but the dynamics and the aims still remain shrouded in mystery, one of many. By chance, did you read the secret report on Vatileaks written by three cardinals, Tomko, Herranz, and De Giorgi, which they delivered only to Ratzinger, who, in turn, handed it on to Francis after his resignation?[22] The famous white box appears in their first photograph at Castel Gandolfo immediately after Bergoglio's election in March 2013. What was in that?

Personally, I never read what that voluminous white box contained, and nothing ever reached the Congregation for the Doctrine of the Faith. Not one page. We were never involved in Vatileaks. I imagine that Paoletto, the majordomo, now deceased, was instrumentalized. I find it surprising that hundreds and hundreds of documents could be stolen from the papal residence under everyone's noses. Is it possible that no one ever noticed anything? My idea is that several individuals in the background who gravitated in the narrow circle of that moment made use of him. They thought Ratzinger was already in the hands of the so-called conservatives and wanted to help him reconstruct another, different image. But they acted in a reckless manner and did enormous damage.

[21] Here, *dimesso*, "resigned."
[22] Here, *dimesso*, "resigned."

You edited the opera omnia of the theologian Ratzinger, collected in sixteen volumes. Do you think his theological thought is destined to leave a mark?

Absolutely, without a shadow of a doubt. He is one of the top theologians, who, already in the seventies, fathomed the crisis of faith and the dynamics of secularization in the Church, analyzing the motives for which the concept of God had been reduced to something worldly, undermined by currents of contemporary philosophy, some even of a nihilist sort. Ratzinger's style of writing theology is inspired by scholars such as Henri de Lubac and Romano Guardini, characterized by a more literary and accessible form that offers a good introduction for today's reader. Take his book *Jesus of Nazareth*, for example: already in the seventies, Ratzinger had shed light on the dangers of a Church sliding down a slope toward transformation into an NGO, massively committed, almost entirely, to social and charitable causes and always less spiritual, neglecting the vertical dimension. In his sermons, he insisted on the simplicity of faith, but never in a reductive sense, and this is important. The problem of our mortality, of hope, of the encounter with Jesus, who looks man in the eyes, constitutes the moment in which humanity can enter into contact with the light of the world.

Do you imagine in the future other popes emeriti, after the path opened by Ratzinger? Pope Francis does not exclude it, in theory — either for himself or for those who will come after him. He has spoken on this various times, even at the beginning of his pontificate.

I expect that the case of Benedict XVI will remain a personal and exceptional case. I have discouraged Pope Francis from following the same path, even though, by character, he always does the opposite of whatever you say to him [*laughs heartily*]. Pope Francis told me that he, too, could have resigned[23] and gone into retirement if certain circumstances were to have come about regarding his health, taking into consideration that Benedict XVI created a precedent, making this hypothesis a possibility to others in the future. Well, opinions on papal resignations[24] are a divisive matter. Remember that Cardinal Maradiaga, a prominent elector of Pope Francis at the conclave (nearly his spokesman), once highly praised Benedict XVI for his resignation.[25]

It is possible that certain sectors of the Church expect the current pontiff to resign,[26] making plans of ecclesial politics pop into their heads, all the better to steer the next conclave, and to identify, who knows, a young candidate in line with the reforms introduced in the meantime. But the Church cannot function this way. Others push for the study of rules that could regulate what should happen to the See of Peter before the natural death of the pontiff. All mechanisms that are destructive of the unity of the Church. Catholics should always accept the elected pope, whoever he is. The first Christians did not say, "I want this one or that one" because common sense told them that ideal men approved by everyone do not exist. Even the Son of God was not loved by all. I don't believe, therefore, there is any use in favoring a club of popes emeriti.

The historical gesture of Benedict XVI should remain an extraordinary gesture and cannot become the rule; it would be harmful for the future. We already have so many obvious problems: one part of the Church identifies with Benedict XVI and another with Francis. Then there is the text of Benedict's renunciation.[27] In my opinion, it contains an erroneous nuance, since the two aspects of the person of the pope,

---

23 Here, *ritirarsi*, "to retreat."

24 Here, *dimissioni*, "resignations."

25 Here, *rinuncia*, "renunciation."

26 Here, *rinunci*, "renounce."

27 Here, *rinuncia*, "renunciation."

the *munus* and the *ministerium*, were kept distinct, whereas they should have remained associated, united. They are inseparable. No one will ever be able to make a law on resignations[28] stating that the pope must leave after a certain number of years or that it's up to his conscience. It's not a question of personal choice, because there are critical implications for the entire Church, with a billion believers involved around the world and more than four thousand bishops. Clearly, one cannot provide the pontiff with directives or commands, but everything must also follow a logic, avoiding an arbitrary modus operandi of "I'll do whatever I want."

Indeed, this does not represent at all the spirituality of the mission of Peter. There exists a theology of the papacy, just as there is a theology of the episcopate. Ratzinger did not have time to reflect on all of this. Perhaps he did not even consult with anyone, and this might have been another error. A consultation with the College of Cardinals might have been too dispersive, a matter of consulting more than two hundred people. But a matter of this sort should have found space for debate, at least with a limited number of people.

As far as you know, does Ratzinger have a sense of guilt for having taken a step backward?

Pope Ratzinger is over ninety-five years old and is happy with his choice, and I'm sure that his disposition was not egoistic. He truly thought that the responsibility was becoming too onerous for him and that a younger man could better face the problems at hand. No one doubted his theological competence, but management issues had emerged over APSA, the IOR,[29] internal bureaucracy, and the growing deficit, making

---

[28] Here, *dimissioni*, "resignations."
[29] The Institute for the Works of Religion (Institutum pro Operibus Religionis).

salary and pension payments difficult. He was not able to follow it all as he would have liked. For this reason, he stepped down.[30]

Over the years, the Mater Ecclesiae Monastery, where Ratzinger has lived since 2013 on the Vatican Hill, has been transformed into a pilgrimage site where people go to heal their souls' wounds, to rediscover a reference point. How did it come to this?

Unfortunately, there are many people who feel wounded by this pontificate. There are various causes. The disruptive effect of the motu proprio *Summa Familiae Cura* of September 8, 2017, comes to mind. In this, Pope Francis suppressed the Pontifical John Paul II Institute, replacing it with the Pontifical John Paul II Theological Institute for the Sciences of Marriage and Family. This academic institute was transformed into another structure; it was distorted, and the consequences cannot be erased, having had repercussions throughout the world. To change or correct the theological line — in this case, concerning the indissolubility of sacramental marriage — it was not necessary to trample natural law, as happened. How is it possible that they fired a professor simply because he did not toe the line of *Amoris Laetitia*, the apostolic exhortation on the family? I'm referring, in particular, to the case of professor Livio Melina, now retired, who, in his entire academic life, had never pronounced a false word against doctrine. Nevertheless, one day, he was suddenly replaced by Archbishop Vincenzo Paglia, who certainly does not have the specific scholarly competence in the sector.

If the independence of professors is not guaranteed in the university setting, clearly chaos will set in sooner or later. Professors have the right to academic freedom in their teaching, and as concerns Catholic doctrine on the family, they cannot be subordinated to trends or to

[30] Here, *lasciato*, "left."

the curial party x or y. Benedict XVI would never have breached this sacrosanct principle of respect and autonomy (in the university). The result is that the number of students now in this new institute has fallen drastically, perhaps to no more than thirty.

In 2013, the elector cardinals gave a precise mandate to Pope Francis: to review Church structures, to bring them back into contact with the faithful, to clean out the rotten apples within, to put into effect the principle of decentralization, and to undertake a program of reforms. In essence, the pontiff is carrying out a program that has been well defined. How might the next conclave unfold?

No conclave can give a mandate to the pope because, once elected, he responds directly to God and not to the cardinals, who certainly have the right to an active electorate, if they have not surpassed their eightieth year, but they are not the ones who transfer pontifical authority. At the moment the newly elected accepts his election, it is Christ who establishes the Successor of Peter. At any rate, a pope cannot obey or respond to the cardinals; the Church does not function like a corporate board of directors. Naturally, it's true that in 2013, there were some serious problems at the IOR as well as in the finances managed by APSA. The electors were worried about a series of scandals, and in the preparatory meetings, they laid out what was needed for the Church to have greater transparency and cleansing. Nevertheless, the newly elected pope is never obliged to follow these pre-electoral programs.

The Church cannot be modernized by the adaptation of secular models, considering that her nature can be ascribed to theological categories and not to political ones. The primary interest remains service to unity. "You are the Son of God" (see Matt. 16:16). The maneuvers that some think they can carry out more or less secretly during the pre-conclave, as if they were functionaries in a political party trying to balance internal factions, have very little to do with a spiritual or theological perception of matters. They act on a secular, pragmatic, worldly vision. Moreover, the activities of the pre-conclave result in preparatory meetings, the so-called novendialis, during which they compare notes and try to analyze the general situation to identify the cardinals to be voted on. But in this, they create initiatives that undermine the configuration of the Church: I'm referring to the attempts of the many lobbies who try to influence the voting. This has always happened. The Community of St. Egidio would like to see its man elected, the Jesuits too, the Salesians as well; the African cardinals work for their candidate. But ontologically speaking, this is wrong. It is God who elects the candidates; this must be the point of departure. The next conclave must take the Church back to her essence, to give emphasis to the principles of the Church and not to the power of ecclesiastical politics.

Can you explain further?

The main challenge the Church faces in the next conclave is to direct her gaze upon the unity of faith and on Jesus Christ. Unfortunately, it's difficult not to notice the increase in the number of bishops around the world who act as if they had forgotten to be pastors interested in eternal life and in the defense of moral principles. It seems to me that they could successfully take up a political career in some political party [*laughs*]. We will need courageous pastors, full of moral integrity and great faith, in the future.

Should bishops stay out of politics?

Certainly, a bishop, a cardinal, and even the pope can carry out political actions. Asserting oneself on political terrain is always a possibility and is also necessary in certain historical moments, but only to remind the world around us of the principles of Christian morality. In the end, it is a parallel action to be developed in the sense of the truth, maintaining autonomy — give unto Caesar what is Caesar's (see Matt. 22:21) — and speaking openly to governments of any stripe, without fear and without hedging. They must avoid aligning with politicians and giving them blatant endorsements before elections, as has happened at times. To the contrary, one should affirm respect for human rights, solidarity, and justice and should denounce corruption and defend morality according to Catholic doctrine.

The second challenge I see on the horizon for the Church concerns the theme of credibility. We pastors, as proclaimers of moral principles, must be the first to live them in complete integrity and transparency. These values are credible and valid per se, independent of those who have to live them out, considering that the Church is composed of fallible men, unfortunately.

The third challenge, on the other hand, is intimately connected to transparency and requires all to act in fidelity to the gospel. It's a matter of adopting, and bringing others to adopt, evangelical models of behavior: I must not steal or succumb to corruption, not so much out of fear of being caught and punished by authorities but because the principle "Thou shalt not steal" is ingrained in me.

Is life after death a given for you? How do you imagine it?

Our death separates us from corporal existence, and this is grievous because man's nature wants to live. For materialists, the afterlife is equated with the absolute end — nothing. But not for Christians, for whom life is a gift from the Lord. And this means that if our existence is not as we would like it to be, no one has the right to suppress it. Abortion and euthanasia should be considered consequences of atheism.

We who believe that after death comes resurrection place our faith in the hands of the Creator. The world, for Christians, cannot be the mere outcome of chaos and chance. God makes us participate in His eternal life. Obviously, we do not know what it will be like in detail, but we know it will be.

And what will Hell be like, then? It probably depends on us, if we deny the Faith or if we live contrary to the good, disfiguring the face of God as love. All depends on freedom. God gave us the freedom to love Him or not to love Him and we do not decide, therefore, who goes to Heaven and who to Hell. The final judgment rests in God's hands. I personally imagine Hell as the total negation of divine love.

Why does the Church no longer speak, as she once did, of the so-called fundamental values: the defense of life from the first instant or marriage between a man and a woman?

On our cultural horizon, there almost seems to be a clash of civilizations on some terrains. On one side are those who defend them; on the other, those who combat them, on the basis of a materialistic idea that reduces man to a being devoid of transcendent horizons. At times, I'm amazed when I listen to bishops and cardinals complain that the Church speaks too much on sexual morality and creates the impression that it is a concentration of prohibitions, when, in reality, it is simply in favor of life. We contrast abortion with the value of the child, from the very moment of the child's conception. These values are fundamental and cannot be relativized, not even in the political sphere, despite a mostly posthuman ideology in which the majority of Western politicians are immersed.

If one speaks of transhumanism and posthumanism as a final consequence of nihilism, it is only because one no longer believes in God; one cannot defend with conviction the human dimension in its totality.

Why was National Socialism so cruel and inhumane? The answer is elementary: because it did not believe in God. In the future, fundamental values must return to the heart of the debate. And we must shout from the rooftops that Christians are in favor of life. For this reason, Christians oppose the advance of euthanasia and abortion. For those with faith, physical or psychological suffering makes sense, above all, when one is ill and reaching the end of one's existence. Believers are called to help the suffering, to visit the sick, to console the afflicted, and to prevent euthanasia. In Holland, where the practice of assisted suicide is more feasible than elsewhere, there are children who tend to convince their elderly parents to end their lives to lighten the burden on the family, to cause fewer problems, to save money. It's perverse. It's as if life for them had no value. And we should not forget that around assisted suicide important economic interests revolve, even if not much is said about them. Focusing on these issues means being criticized as politically incorrect.

Do you remember Msgr. Krzysztof Charamsa, your colleague at the Congregation for the Doctrine of the Faith who, in 2015, made his "coming out," announcing to the world that he was gay and wanting to move to Barcelona to live with a companion? Since you knew him, were you aware of the move he was about to make?

Of course I remember him. He was a very intelligent and well-prepared colleague; I even promoted him as assistant to the International Theological Commission. I had contact with him until the moment of his coming out, but since then, I have not heard from him. I found out what had happened from the TV, although the previous day, someone had mentioned to me that Charamsa wanted to make his public declaration. I couldn't believe it. It was the start of the synod on *Amoris Laetitia*, and certainly his provocatory stance was agreed upon (I don't know by whom) to exercise a type of public pressure on the Church in favor of gay couples. I confess I was disappointed. It was a blow for the Vatican and for the Congregation for the Doctrine of the Faith — and also for me, since I had good relations with him. I had been kept in the dark, but I could not have controlled every detail of the private life of those who work in that dicastery. Nevertheless, I can say that Charamsa, during his years in the Vatican, was always upright and competent.

Does a gay lobby exist in the Vatican?

I remember that the pope spoke of this at the start of his pontificate. It's said they are the favorites in the Vatican. No one has ever come to me with specific requests, and I know no one belonging to this lobby. In any case, homosexuality should not be admitted among priests, in seminaries, or in the Vatican. Of everyone is demanded maturity, rectitude in their private as well as their public lives.

The case of the former American cardinal and pedophile Theodore Mc-Carrick caused an uproar in the United States. During the pontificate of Benedict XVI, the then apostolic nuncio to the United States, Carlo Maria Viganò, served McCarrick with the papal order to retreat from public life. The response of the Washington archbishop was to continue to behave as if nothing had happened, confident in the fact that he was one of the major benefactors of the Curia and the Holy See. The punishment arrived only later with Pope Francis when charges by minors reached the Vatican, but not due to homosexual acts with young seminarians. Is that how things went?

No charges of pedophilia against him reached the Congregation for the Doctrine of the Faith, at least when I was there. Only later was the case presented in that form. There was gossip about McCarrick, for sure. I'm referring to voices without details that told of homosexual relations with young seminarians — adults, though. Gossip and chatter. Only later did true charges arise. In any case, the pope, any pope, cannot take care of everything; it is inconceivable. The first to act should be collaborators who, with autonomy, have the task to act for the good of the Church, according to truth and justice. What am I referring to? If gossip is going around or if there are detailed complaints, inspection must be immediately undertaken on the part of the Congregation of Bishops to understand if those complaints are well founded or if they are only calumny. From that point, action can be taken. I did not know the archbishop of Washington personally; I had seen him only once.

Pope Francis later used a heavy hand with McCarrick. In the end, he removed his cardinal status and removed him from the clerical state, recognizing his guilt in abuses against minors.

Only in the end was something done. Even Andrea Tornielli confirmed in an article that McCarrick had been condemned and punished because he abused an underage adolescent but not for the other relations with adult seminarians and consenting adults. It seems a strange line of argument to me. A bishop, in fact, is always bound to give good example and consequently must not have sexual relations with anyone — certainly not with seminarians, consenting adults. These things do harm. The problem is that perhaps moral theology in the Church has been sent into the attic. One uses other thought categories, influenced by the weight of public opinion, according to which relations among adult men are considered licit. For the Church, though, these are grave sins. There is no justification for a bishop who has had sexual relations with adults.

Why does no one recognize this moral deviation? It is the mirror of relativism, of the secularization of Christian thought and, certainly, one cannot accept that public opinion decides what is or is not grave sin. It is divine law that defines this. Every Christian is responsible for his conscience before God. McCarrick, who always made his liberal ideas known publicly, had a heavy influence in the United States and also in China. He was generous and donated much money to the Vatican. I was amazed by how many people in the Curia benefited personally from this; a list was even published in the United States. I don't know if this could be defined as a form of modern simony; perhaps it was truly about supporting religious works. Who can know? Maybe there should be a prohibition against bishops who come to Rome bringing money as gifts to prefects of the Curia. Better if all of this is registered and traced.

Did this happen to you as well?

This never happened to me, especially because they said: "Müller is German and therefore wealthy and has no need of money" [*laughs heartily*].

The Church and the Future

What are the big theological questions still open that should be faced immediately by the next pope?

Christian faith will have to be worked on. The challenge posed by nihilism and atheism constitutes the source in which totalitarian ideologies have always set down their roots. The lack of a true religion, of a living relationship with God, has left in society a large vacuum filled by a certain background desperation. Politics, as important as it is, has not been capable of giving meaning to people's lives and of explaining theologically the mystery of being. We Christians, by now a minority, are capable of resisting.

Do you include the environment and the climate question among the challenges the Church of the future will have to deal with, considering the social encyclical **Laudato Si'***?*

Although it is not considered part of classical theology, the theme of the environment enters fully into theology because it is God who entrusted creation to man to allow him to enjoy its fruits and to make it grow in harmony with other living beings, and certainly not to have him pursue his own interests, exploiting indiscriminately a common patrimony. *Laudato Si'* is an important document to Francis's pontificate, and in some ways, it can be compared to *Rerum Novarum*. In the text, however, there are no absolute theological innovations, because the discussion underway over this enormous topic, as well as the adoption of the principles of creation or the framing of the concept of integral ecology, moves within an already established framework. It remains a document of relevant importance and should be studied in school. In the future, we will need an integral ecology invested with humanist principles.

When one speaks of a wide-ranging ecological conversion, the intention is not to introduce a sort of *pietà* with respect to the environment but to solicit across-the-board action from below that touches all humanity. This is a favored line of encounter with Christ, aimed at seeking solutions for the salvation of the species in danger from the Anthropocene. If one respects nature, one must respect the life of man as well, from beginning to end.

Which challenges do you foresee in particular?

The biggest challenge is tied to transhumanism — the cultural movement that affirms technological and scientific modernity to obtain physical and physiological benefits for the human species; for example, health improvements, lengthened life spans, the strengthening of intellectual and social capacities. We Christians cannot make statements such as: "We have nothing against this, so let the people do whatever they want." The Church must necessarily express herself on this subject. It's a matter of guarding human dignity and the meaning of its existence and not only concentrating on the interests that revolve around this question. This is our mission.

There are other challenges connected to this, regarding technological frontiers. Technology has a good goal. However, it is conditioned by ethics applied to it in order to make out of it a marvelous, positive instrument, rather than something harmful. It's the eternal difference between good and evil, which does not depend on technology as such but on the moral principles applied to it. The Church will have to learn to speak more openly, even if this will not please many financial potentates and politicians — above all, Catholic ones, who will have to be recalled to the truth of faith and not only think about the next electoral appointment.

Certainly, one of the great challenges the cardinals will have to face in the next conclave concerns the Church and the division between a wealthy world on one side and a direly poor one on the other.

Thousands of the richest and most influential people in the world meet at Davos regularly. This group of people alone holds 95 percent of the planet's wealth. Important prospects have been considered in this context, capable of restyling the world and determining the compass to follow in the immediate future. I think a distorted conscience has materialized, characterized by the propensity of the wealthiest to cultivate philanthropic attitudes to control the masses (for example, when they spoke of giving everyone a universal income). Even Stalin, in his time, affirmed that we are all equal and everyone should be given the same possibilities. Why do I return to this historical reference? All of us have the noble and primary goal of indicating the way to rid the world of inequality, injustice, and hunger and to have an effect on social inequality. Has anyone at Davos ever asked who is responsible for all the misery on the planet? Going back two centuries, during colonialism, our leaders became rich by exploiting lands in Africa or in Latin America. Now these people appear in other clothes. Take one of the richest men on the planet, Jeff Bezos. He became a billionaire through corporate structures whose working conditions do not always seem to shine with integrity, farsightedness, and social cohesion. The Church's social doctrine states that extraordinary wealth must be equitably distributed. Every worker has the right to a fair salary for his labor and to fixed rest. It is intolerable that a worker receives a thousand Euros at the end of the month while his boss receives two million Euros: even a child can see that this is a disparity to be rectified. This is a case of collective labor. The Church's social doctrine insists on the fact that the profit must be distributed in just proportion.

Marx said that too.

Yes, but he came eighteen hundred years after Christ. Our Lord was the first to talk about the super rich. He sided immediately with the poor. He criticized the powerful and those who exploit their power for their own glory and not for the good of the people. Julius Caesar had great notoriety and was an excellent strategist, but how many people had to die because of his lust for conquest? The same is true of Napoleon. There is always a double standard. Ex-Chancellor Angela Merkel invited Bill Gates to discuss vaccination against Covid, and she did well, but it cannot be said that during her term in office, she had the exact same enthusiasm for common people. Because of coronavirus, millions of people around the world lost their jobs and plunged into poverty, while a handful of super rich became even more affluent than before and actually doubled their worth during the pandemic, as the *Forbes* statistics demonstrate. How much longer can this be tolerated? I think this is not normal, and it is certainly unjust to accept it, at least on the part of the Church: it remains unjustifiable. It is possible to affirm that Liberation Theology developed from the social doctrine and, in particular, from conciliar texts.

Throughout history, various tendencies hostile to Christianity have arisen: secularism, materialism, postmodernism, transhumanism, extreme liberalism, and atheism. Where does the greatest danger for the Church lie?

Without a doubt, once more in transhumanism, which, in reality, is anti-humanism. As I have stated, the word *transhumanism* refers to a school of thought that seeks the improvement of the human condition carried out by exceeding the biological limits of our bodies through the use of the intellect and scientific innovation. At the moment, the ethical dilemmas this creates or will introduce are not being considered: I'm referring to the vision of a hypothetical "beyond human." But if man's partnership with God, his point of reference in God, is lost, man will lose himself and, in the end, has no need of redemption for his sins. He wants to get beyond mortality. This places transhumanism as the consequence of atheism; it means that man has no need for God as the cause and origin of his being but believes only in a personal God made for himself. It is obvious that this line of thought cannot go far: we have seen what happened to communism in Russia and China. The Communist Party became a sort of divinity, an end in itself. They even distorted the idea of Marx. It worries me when a philosophical vision takes over that transforms humanity into an abstract, to the point of assuming totalitarian forms of control over humanity.

In this deviant manipulation of the masses I would place the super rich who frequent Davos. They pay sixty thousand Euros to enter the forum so they can take part in the elaboration of future strategies for the world. Normal people, the middle class, small businessmen, on the other hand, are excluded. The elite appear in a selective way, quasi-autocratic, and speak for the collectivity, promoting ideas that are often manipulatory, for the salvation of the world, the planet, the human race. As such, their ideas are not bad in this conceptual perspective. Even Stalin said he based his action on positive theoretical assumptions; he, too, wanted to save the masses and humanity. Hitler also insinuated himself into the folds of history as a messiah. In China, however, the mechanism concerns, above all, the current president, Xi, a sort of divinity for some time now. The Chinese obliged everyone to memorize a book containing his ideas, his thoughts, his writings, even though Xi is not a philosopher. Given this premise, I'm convinced there are no new concepts. The temptation to create a new world and govern the masses existed before Davos. Even Napoleon said he wanted to construct a new Europe. I consider this to be a cyclic reality, a consequence that manifests itself when people stop believing in the power of God, Creator and Redeemer.

How do you imagine the Church in the future? Can you synthesize possible fields of action?

In the world today, we witness dynamics fomented by a capitalism that controls the masses — a minority of the super rich that oversees the majority — that cannot last long. A different horizon can be found in the gospel, which offers a solid base, founded on the ability to remain human, to defend the dignity of the person and guarantee his future. This might seem obvious, yet just look at the challenges raised by modern medicine and artificial intelligence. We can identify positive aspects obviously, but only if they become instruments of growth and not of dominion of some men over others.

Seneca says: "Most people, lacking a compass, always change their minds, prey to a voluble and unstable lightness and dissatisfied with themselves." Where is the West going? Toward a vision that sees man without God or man in a peer relationship with God?

We Christians have a different viewpoint from pagan philosophy, even if Seneca can be considered a reference figure, often placed next to St. Paul for a series of temporal coincidences. When the Stoicism of Seneca flourished in Rome, Christianity had already permeated the empire and was spreading. For us Christians, God is the God of revelation, while for Seneca, God was the basis of human nature, almost a personal divinity. The passage about the burning bush, in which God revealed Himself to Moses, comes to mind. This is the key scene to understanding the religion of the Old Testament. The self-awareness of the person is derived from this, not only as creation but as the image of the absolute principle of being.

The process of de-Christianization began only in the eighteenth century with the Enlightenment, which denied elements of Christianity to the point of reducing it to natural religion. There were thinkers such as Herbert of Cherbury who came to an openly atheistic vision, denying the existence of God. Julien Offray de La Mettrie, Dietrich d'Holbach, Darwin. The school of reductionism brought about the elaboration of the concept of the masses by other authors, and Yuval Noah Harari comes to mind here. He writes that man is nothing more than a computer program, in a setting where the body, the sentiments, can be transcended, and what remains is formal intelligence. This is the final leap of human evolution, a step toward hyperintelligence almost entirely artificial. And it's a perspective in which the Jeff Bezos types proliferate, cultivating the idea that man can attain a sort of immortality, not as a gift of God but as self-proclamation through technology. Man as God or the man-God. It's the final stage of a path that negates Christianity.

You often evoke the fear of the so-called Great Reset, a proposal of the World Economic Forum of Davos to reconstruct the economy in a sustainable way after the Covid-19 pandemic. It was presented in May 2020 jointly by then Prince of Wales Charles and the director of the World Economic Forum, Klaus Schwab. What about it does not convince you?

I see a lot of ambiguity in the world due in large part to the limits of the Enlightenment and to the confident outlook of constructing a social reality without pain, anguish, or the fear of death, while the idea of reducing man to a machine is reinforced. Again, Harari's book *Homo Deus* is enlightening. I find emblematic the thesis he proposes based on the notion that having a soul is no longer relevant, given that we are in a crucial phase in human evolution. In practice, man's individuality is negated, affirming as an illusion the need for personal resurrection as a fundamental part of our identity. Artificial intelligence will be the vehicle of a new world consisting of pure technology, until this brings about an artificial intelligence no longer individual.

Harari's thesis heavily influenced the leaders at Davos, where they spoke of the theory of the so-called Great Reset. At this international gathering, they also analyzed how to create a common horizon in which the individual is nearly entirely regulated. In this regard, a phrase by the visionary entrepreneur Elon Musk made me reflect. He said that the world of the future would no longer need workers. The problem is what will become of this mass of men who will have no need of employment. It was said that a universal income would be guaranteed to all. In reality, this vision does not match at all with that of the Church, even if Pope Francis is not opposed to the idea, perhaps because he comes from Latin America, a continent marked by situations of extreme poverty — where approaches such as these (of a Peronist stripe) are more effective. It's like saying, "We'll give money to all to fight and defeat poverty."

But the universal income does not work for the social doctrine of the Church, which, instead, sustains the right to work with one's own hands and thus to support one's family. The universal income winds up being a sort of gift and renders dependent those who receive it, creating economic control over the masses. The theory of the Great Reset, advanced by the economist Klaus Schwab, describes an economy in the hands of stakeholders and proposes a structure more equitable and more sustainable of the environment and exploits the innovations of the Fourth Industrial Revolution — that is, the improvement of capitalism with investments aimed at reciprocal progress.

Naturally, everything gets decided by a very few, and the democratic dimension disappears. This dynamic seems quite similar to the way in which the Communist Party once defined what might be the happiness of its citizens. The Church must not give in to these ideas, must not accept them. At their core, there lies an innovative, materialistic anthropology that risks undermining the Church's action, reducing it to an NGO like any other.

Is happiness possible for the man of today?

Aristotle states that happiness is the choice that makes one well. I am happy under certain conditions — for example, if I am free of illnesses, of accidents, if I have good friends, if I enjoy freedom of thought. For the Christian, happiness consists in having found God, the love of God. At this point, the question arises whether those who do not believe in God are condemned to be unhappy people, depressed, overcome. Often one thinks that the meaning of a happy life consists only in wealth: that to become a millionaire or to own a yacht or a huge mansion might be the measure of happiness. We Christians are convinced that material goods are insufficient. Aristotle adds that happiness cannot be placed only in wealth, but to do the good as such. Jesus does not talk as much of happiness as He does of blessedness, and this is not a matter of subjective, ephemeral happiness but being full of the presence of God and of the Spirit of God. The possession of material goods alone certainly cannot satisfy man and his tendency toward a more precious reality. One who has millions has a high probability of being unhappy if he is deprived of friends, of family, of affections. The spirit, the soul, the interior gaze toward the absolute cannot be neglected because man shall not live on bread alone, but on every word that proceeds from the mouth of God, says Jesus (see Matt. 4:4). He might lack many material things and yet still can be full of joy on account of his family and the affection and love he can give and receive. The love that makes us always happy, however, is not enough in itself because the one who has no food for his children cannot feel joy. Faith and charity cannot be separated. This is why in the Our Father we pray for our daily bread and then we say, "Thy kingdom come," introducing the transcendent perspective.

The Question of Women

To this point, you have never cited a female theologian. Is it possible there are no important female theologians?

No, there were not many women theologians in the past. In the list, though, one would certainly include Edith Stein, Teresa of Ávila, and Hildegard of Bingen, among the more famous. Unfortunately, Edith Stein did not have the opportunity to complete her studies because she was killed by Nazis in a concentration camp. Today there are interesting and promising female theologians; for example Hanna-Barbara Gerl-Falkovitz. In the International Theological Commission there are various female scholars.

Hildegard and Teresa were proclaimed Doctors of the Church.

Wouldn't it be better to call them "Doctoresses" of the Church?

I wouldn't say so. The Latin noun is *Doctor*.

In Germany, reflection within the Church has been undertaken in which a substantial revision of the role of women in the Church, including sacramental functions, is being requested. A commission to evaluate the possibility of admitting female deacons was instituted in the Vatican — a debate that has gone on indecisively since the time of Paul VI. Various pontiffs, including Pope Francis, have explained the impossibility for women to be admitted to all three degrees of the sacrament of Ordination. Do you imagine the possibility of changes in this direction in the future?

The question is open on female deacons, but as concerns the sacrament of Ordination, from the theological point of view, I would say the road is closed. From the very beginning, this ministry has been reserved to men. The explanation can be synthetized in an image: they represent Christ the Bridegroom of the Church, and precisely this sacramental dimension constitutes the clear sign, and this role cannot be changed. There is no discrimination behind this. Only a man can present Christ as Bridegroom, which does not mean that women cannot have greater managerial space than they already do. Nevertheless, if we consider the theological essence, it becomes clear that we cannot proceed in this direction. Unfortunately, most people think only in functionalist categories, as if the Church were a state or a multinational, neglecting the sacrament of Holy Orders.

Clearly, the question must be framed in another way. The connection with Christ the Bridegroom and His Church, as mentioned before, must be the point of departure. No man could become the cause and origin of the Incarnation because only of a woman can the Son of God as man be born. It is not even possible to transform this expression, which is not a privilege but the fundamental principle of the natural order — just as a man cannot wed another man; it would be against the foundation of creation. The sacrament, therefore, is a visible sign elevated to an instrument of grace. The two sacraments — Holy Orders and Matrimony — are in relation to the man and the woman. Women can, without a doubt, become heads of state or lead an army, and they can certainly do so better than men.

From a theological point of view, however, the priesthood is not considered; otherwise, we end up not understanding that the Church is much, much more than a state; it is the mirror of the divine. It is misleading, therefore, to think of introducing different criteria, as if it were a business, a corporation, because it would have nothing to do with the perspective of salvation in Christ. It is obvious that for public opinion, it is easier to accept the Church as a social organization than as an instrument of salvation. Here we see the difficulty in understanding that it is not possible to erase the Church's transcendent, spiritual character. The secular current will always struggle to accept the sacred aspect of the Church, linked to life after death and the mystery of the Trinity.

In the German synodal way and elsewhere, one speaks of the great question of women and the fact that, for centuries, women in the Church have been excluded and discriminated against. Perhaps this is a disparity that should be corrected, don't you think?

As such, the question is poorly framed, given that Baptism renders us all equal, male and female. This is the first error we make when speaking of the Church, which (I reiterate it always when I hold conferences before a non-Catholic audience) is the communion of the faithful in divine grace. From this assumption, the requests for women's priesthood are not an exclusion. The priesthood is not an exercise issued by a political power, and for this reason we cannot give it a false representation. It is, instead, a ministry born to serve all and to lead humanity to eternal salvation. Christ established that men would be His disciples and would become His successors. I wonder why the women's question has concentrated so much on this single aspect: it's not that women have value only when they have power over others. Mary had no sacramental power, and the same goes for the great female saints and mystics, beginning with St. Catherine and St. Teresa.

Don't you think there's an enormous open wound, considering the predominant chauvinism in the Church?

Honestly, I do not believe the Church is male chauvinist, in the true sense of the word. That's one of the many prejudices that circulate. There are no obstacles, in fact, to women's holding academic roles at the highest levels, such as professors of theology in pontifical universities. So, too, could they aspire to senior positions in the Secretariat of State or elsewhere in the Curia. Naturally, to be a professor of theology, precise competencies are required.

Women can occupy all positions in the Church that are not connected to the sacrament of Ordination. I consider feasible, for example, the nomination of a woman as apostolic nuncio or as secretary of state or even as a substitute for the deputy for general affairs or the governor of the IOR. Perhaps the moment has arrived for a female secretary of state or head of the governorate, seeing that these are positions open to laypeople as well, without any preclusions. But regarding the priesthood, there is an insurmountable limit: a priest can only be a man, just as for the cardinalate. This is inconceivable for a woman because at the origin of the College of Cardinals, there was the link with priesthood, such that every church in Rome is still associated with a cardinal. Furthermore, it was Pope John XXIII who established that cardinals had to be ordained bishops, although Alfredo Ottaviani, then prefect of the Holy Office, was a simple priest at the moment he was elevated to the cardinalate.

In the future, could there be room for a qualified female presence among the electors called to elect the pope in a conclave?

To understand the direction to take, we need to start from the roots, from the beginning. The conclave began to take form when the Church of Rome started to elect its bishop, the Successor of Peter. It was not an election in the democratic sense but a choice guided by the Holy Spirit. Later, the limits and rules were slowly defined until we arrived at today's situation. We know that in the Middle Ages, and even later, there were important noble families who lobbied to influence the choice of the successor. It was Niccolò II who established the first rules for the election, and from there, the norms were perfected up until the current constitution, *Universi Dominici Gregis*. It was clarified that only the cardinals of the Roman Church — those incardinated in the titular churches — have the right to vote, in order to limit chaos and external pressure.

Cultural conditions have changed throughout the centuries, though.

We cannot always react to ongoing cultural and social changes. Our anthropology is based on biology and the concept of the person; the human being is a person. We cannot contrast a theological vision with a cultural one. The fact remains that human beings were created male and female, a clear biological foundation. It follows that so-called gender theory is erroneous and false because human beings can be only male or female. It is not possible to change one's sex at birth.

So, for you, there's no unresolved women's question in the Church?

In the future, it will certainly be dealt with better, but it depends on one's point of view. Love and power: these are the two reference terms for elaborating a new path. The compass. We can also analyze, of course, the theme of violence, abuse of power, and so forth, affirming that, according to the gospel, no human being of the male sex can exercise power over women. Next to the theme of power, there is also that of love, love that leads to growth and signifies that God made us equal. To reconsider the practical implications, we must take this parity as our starting point.

Women continue to be excluded even from the diaconate, an issue under consideration since the time of Paul VI.

I've written three books on this subject. The questions have been clarified. We have a unity in the sacraments that cannot be divided. That's not possible; it would be a contradiction. Nevertheless, there are studies that give concrete value to women. But women deacons are not foreseen in the sacramental structure of priestly Ordination.

In the Church, delays in recognizing the importance of women are evident. Take the case of Hildegard of Bingen, mystic, scientist, theologian, composer, musician, philosopher, and politician. Her genius is widely evident throughout her vast works. She was counselor to Frederick Barbarossa in an age marked by the backwardness of the condition of women. Her greatness, however, was only recently discovered: John Paul II beatified her, and Benedict XVI finally did her justice by proclaiming her a Doctor of the Church and a saint. Is Hildegard perhaps an example of the unresolved women's question?

True, around the world, Hildegard was never very well known, but in Germany she has always been held in high regard by theologians and venerated as a saint by the faithful, well before her canonization. Her works are studied and translated, and the Monastery of Eibingen, about nine miles from where I grew up, is known by all, a very famous site. On the world level, her stature has long remained relegated to the academic sphere: only specialists recognized the depth of her thought. Nevertheless, she is a magnificent mystic. In the past, few other women have had similar roles. Macrina, the sister of Basil the Great, and Catherine of Siena come to mind. But they can be counted on one hand, whereas the Doctors of the Church and the Church Fathers are many. The delay with Hildegard was reconciled with Benedict XVI. As a German, he knew her well and appreciated her philosophical and theological approach, which the medieval mystic developed concerning God — God is love. Consequently, Ratzinger recognized in Hildegard her innovative thought, close to his own and inspiring to him.

Violence and abuse of women are more widespread than it might seem in every part of the world. Could the reason be traced back to the patriarchal cultural model borrowed by the Church as well, and do you think that, in the future, this issue could be addressed with more conviction than it has been thus far?

Violence should never be a matter of speculation: violence is evil. No one can abuse, wound, strike, or manipulate another person, be that person man or woman. This is an expression of Original Sin that develops when a human being starts to dominate and exploit another. As is comprehensible, this issue has seen a cultural evolution over the course of centuries: four thousand years ago, there were no sociologists studying how to better organize the community, and no one noticed the existence of disparity between the sexes. Take the scourge of slavery. In Athens, there were slaves, as there were in Rome, where slavery was more or less tolerated for a long time. The global slave trade from Africa was weakened only toward the end of the nineteenth century. Christianity promotes an idea based on equality of persons. Unfortunately, it does not always have the power to change the world according to its principles. The Church is against war, and yet war continues to sow death. This is to say that violence against women is part of a structural root and requires us to work seriously to eradicate it. I know there exists violence against women in the Church, but it is a limited problem. These are cases that go against doctrine, grave sins not in conformity with the will of God. Nonetheless, I consider it a complex issue that should be given greater attention by everyone.

The Americas

In the United States, the bishops are divided over ethical questions — in particular, Communion for pro-abortion politicians. Pope Francis cautioned against dragging such topics into the political field, but the archbishop of San Francisco, Salvatore Cordileone, went so far as to ask Speaker of the House Nancy Pelosi to renounce "publicly her convictions"; otherwise, he wrote, "she cannot consider herself a Catholic and cannot receive Communion." President Joe Biden, a Catholic, also risked being banned from the Sacrament by the more conservative American bishops for his pro-abortion positions, but the pontiff intervened on his behalf. What is the Magisterium's position?

The archbishop of San Francisco prohibited Nancy Pelosi from [receiving] Communion precisely for the support she gave to legislation favorable to abortion. Unfortunately, the bishops in the United States are not all of the same opinion. The archbishop of San Diego, Robert McElroy, who was actually promoted by the pope to the cardinalate at the consistory in late August 2022, affirms that Communion remains a private matter and that the Church must avoid clashes with politicians. This is a falsity. Receiving Communion is never an action aimed at satisfying one's personal religious sentiments. It is the Real Presence of Jesus, communion with the entire Church. It's a sacrament, not a social rite. Faith and one's private life ought to coincide, walk together in harmony. This must be true for Catholic politicians as well. No one is obliging them to defend the principles of the Church. They are required, however, to protect the natural law, which includes the unconditional value of human life.

The Congregation for the Doctrine of the Faith, in turn, has clarified these issues so that all may easily understand them. It has stated that Catholic politicians cannot cooperate directly or indirectly in pro-abortion legislative texts insofar as they deny the precept "Thou shalt not kill," a commandment written in man's conscience. St. Paul writes that the decalogue is sculpted in hearts and in the conscience (see Rom. 2:15). Regretfully, one must observe, some of Pope Francis's stances have not always been clear in this regard and have contributed to obfuscating the question. With President Trump, for example, the pontiff affirmed that building a border wall between Mexico and the United States was not Christian. Obviously, we're all in agreement. But then with President Biden, a convinced abortion supporter, in order to avoid a direct clash with the White House, he allows him to receive Communion. This is a contradiction. The drama of abortion splits, divides, lacerates. If a bishop accepts the Catholic Faith, he can never be in favor of the interruption of a pregnancy or of those politicians who indulge it with their orientation or their votes.

Unfortunately, we cannot construct the unity of the episcopate — in this case, the American episcopate — to the detriment of Christian truth. It would be a mistake. Faith in Christ requires integrity, acceptance of the revealed truth, rigor toward the natural and moral law. If there are bishops who give Communion to Biden or Pelosi to enjoy good political relations with them, it is a terrible incoherence. In the time of Arianism as well, when Arius said that Christ was only a primary creature of God but not consubstantial with the Father, the Church was dramatically split, and the majority of bishops were Arian. No episcopate will ever be able to find a synthesis while negating the divinity of Christ.

Pope Francis was heavily criticized by Catholics in the United States for having crossed the line of appropriate neutrality with President Joe Biden. Was their reaction exaggerated?

Everyone is free to cultivate personal biases — and in this, I refer to the attitude Francis had in the past with respect to President Trump — but the fact remains that at the moment of his election, a pope assumes a nonpartisan role; he represents the unity of the Church; he is the Successor of Peter. In some situations, Francis seems to have acted more on the basis of preconceived notions or political calculations. I could even advance explanations of a sociological sort, such as the reality frequent among South Americans of harboring an innate aversion toward North Americans — the Gringos. Perhaps the root is diffidence, but I wouldn't know. The higher interest of the Vicar of Christ is the task of illuminating everyone, of speaking with frankness and clarity and never closing the doors to anyone.

The pope has also been criticized regarding the war in Ukraine. Many observers have had the impression that he came down on the side of the Russians, perhaps for the noble goal of opening a window of dialogue. Do you agree with this reading?

The pope has offered strong words for the sake of a ceasefire; he has made appeals and has sought to do everything possible for the refugees, even though he has never openly condemned Putin since the beginning of the conflict. There was probably fear that the Kremlin might vindicate itself on the lives of the Catholic communities present in Russian territory: it is a small minority, though very lively and active. When the war broke out, perhaps he could have addressed the Russian president publicly, taking advantage of the fact that Putin is a practicing Christian and pointing out that kissing icons and lighting candles in the Muscovite Cathedral of Christ the Redeemer should have led him to reflect on the gospel, preventing him from the deliberate killing of tens of thousands of Ukrainians and the destruction of cities, in an incessant propaganda compromised by lies. How can a Christian who goes to church succumb to such violence, and how can this contradiction be explained? In my opinion, President Putin, precisely because he is a practicing Orthodox Christian, constitutes an example even worse than figures such as Hitler and Stalin, considering that they were both atheists. From a Christian who presents himself in public using Christian symbols — for example, the rosary or the crucifix — one expects an attitude in conformity with Christian principles.

Is war morally acceptable when it's a matter of combating to defend one's territory from an aggressor?

No war is "just." Every type of war is opprobrious. A defensive war exists to the extent to which the life of one's people and one's own land, unjustly invaded, must be guaranteed. Killing a man in legitimate defense remains abominable but morally permissible. Even the term *justify* is improper, and I would not use it. A war cannot be justified, only tolerated, and within a tight framework of conditions. The motives for which one defends oneself can be considered just, however.

Beginning with Thomas and Augustine, a long tradition of theological evaluation exists. Even in the Old Testament, something of this can be found. In any case, conflicts are never to be involved with the concept of "holy." We can accept it in the face of brutal aggression and after having put into effect every diplomatic instrument possible. It is licit, however, to arm a country that is defending itself, and that cannot be a theoretical exercise. How else could a country under attack defend itself from an aggressor without weapons? Think of the case of Kiev and Moscow. Catholic pacifists do not approve of the giving of arms to the Ukrainians. There has been much controversy, but we need to make it known to them that if they don't agree with the doctrine of the Church, they can always choose to submit to President Putin. They can also move to Siberia if they want to work without wages for Moscow. At times, the lack of knowledge of Catholic doctrine is abysmal.

If someone enters a house, occupies the rooms, and kills some of the children, will the father say, "I can't do anything, and I don't want to defend myself"? What would happen to the other children still there who risk being killed? What are the Russians doing in Ukraine? They are killing thousands of people and destroying infrastructure, and the Church cannot accept what is happening. It's another matter to give a blessing to soldiers at the front with a gesture deprived of sacrality, done with affection and hoping the soldiers will survive. Nevertheless, it leaves room for ambiguity. The *Catechism* talks about the right to self-defense of peoples, but the matter concerning atomic weapons remains unresolved, and the destructive potential raises enormous doubts and leads into the unknown.

Is the Church destined to become irrelevant in politics and in society in the near future?

The Church's relevance must be the gospel and the truth of the gospel, even if it should reach the point of dividing a family: on one side, those for Christ; on the other, those against Him. At any rate, suffice it to recall the Gospel saying "Do not think that I have come to bring peace on earth; I have not come to bring peace, but a sword" (Matt. 10:34). It means that divine truth is a challenge for us, that it is really not comfortable to be a Christian. Living according to one's own interests is comfortable enough, yet Christianity brings with it a certain upheaval of things, and true peace comes only when we accept the saving will of God. The Church must be able to exercise her own action in politics, not for strategic or material advantage but to defend — shouting from the rooftops — the Ten Commandments. Sometimes bizarre and contradictory things happen.

You studied and collaborated at length with Liberation Theology; in theory, you could be described as a communist.

[*Laughs.*] You know, I've been called a communist a number of times. If anything, I am a "communionist," from *communio*, a Latin term borrowed from a somewhat conservative Peruvian archbishop during my sojourn in Lima.

What memories do you have of the period you spent in Latin America?

Wonderful personal memories and an experience that allowed me to make an in-depth analysis of the Church. In light of recent history, there has been a tendency to radicalize the position of the Latin American Church: on one side, those who drew near to the Right and, on the other, the extremists of the Left. The Church did not have a sufficient antidote within and was not able to identify the danger immediately and to fight so as not to be overwhelmed. In analogous situations, the risk is to transform every activity into an exercise of power that undermines Christian credibility from the base.

I had the good fortune to have had a lengthy collaboration with the theologian Gustavo Gutiérrez. We wrote three books together. Liberation Theology is an important current of thought that was nourished by Vatican II and highlights the values of social and political emancipation present in the Christian message, as well as emphasizes the preferential option for the poor, as found in Scripture. It's an idea, therefore, that goes beyond extreme capitalism and extreme socialism.

How did this strong friendship with the Peruvian theologian Gustavo Gutiérrez come about?

A dear friend. We shared a long human and academic path. I met him in 1988 in Peru, at a theological conference on Liberation Theology. Together, we published three books on the theme of poverty, formulating critiques on unrestrained capitalism not anchored in the Church's social doctrine. Whoever holds that this theological movement is an old tool of the Left makes a big mistake and shows a lack of thorough understanding of it. It should be taken up again and reconsidered for its farsightedness. In the past, problems were created, unfortunately, by some decidedly naive Latin American ecclesiastics: they held that communism was the solution to some of the problems of that age. This was the period of Castro, Che Guevara, and Camilo Torres, the first priest who altered the theological course of Liberation Theology, affirming that one could preach Christ and at the same time carry a gun and fight for the revolution of justice. These were absurd ideas. Liberation Theology develops the analysis of social problems by applying Christian anthropology. The point of departure is the social assumption, pregnant with fractures and injustice, characterized by the discrepancy between those who have too much and those who do not even have enough to feed their children. Many of the ideas of Liberation Theology are found in *Gaudium et Spes*, the conciliar document that inspired it.

What do you mean by "super capitalism"?

[I mean] when, in a business, profit is the only parameter, and they do not consider at all that those who work in the business are responsible for corporate life, under the light of collective labor. Super capitalism recalls Liberation Theology and the preferential option for the poor, whose roots of validity are in the gospel. For the Church, the poor are those who are insignificant, "nonpeople" to whom the fullness of human rights is not recognized. Basically, without social or individual importance, they generally count very little in society. Certainly, the economic issue is fundamental, but it is not the only one.

The reasons the poor are not "seen" are various: without a doubt, the lack of money, but also the color of their skin, being a woman, being part of a despised culture. Poverty is a multifaceted complex of factors. This approach suggests cultivating a new outlook, solidarity of all toward all, in a continual flow. Marxists have always leveled harsh criticism at the Church for being a supporter of the privileged classes. This obviously does not correspond to the truth. Just think of the social works that have been carried out through the centuries, starting with *Rerum Novarum*, and which still bear fruit today: rural banks; cooperative banks; assistance to factory workers, to field workers, to children in families in difficulty; associations of mutual assistance.

The Church has always defended private property, though under certain conditions. In the future, if the widening gap between the richest (ever richer) and the poor (ever poorer) is not halted, from the theological point of view, could the issue be turned on its head and perhaps canceled as a guaranteed right?

Private property remains for the Church the material basis for freedom. Nevertheless, some limits must exist. Private property cannot continue over the deprivation of others. In a capitalist system, there are some who get rich at the expense of others without taking responsibility of any kind, and there are no limits to private property. Communism, to the contrary, foresees a system of severe control; the party takes care of everything. According to the Church, therefore, property is not an absolute in principle, nor is it a relative aspect. To enjoy freedom, one needs money, food, and a roof over one's head. There can be no freedom where a heavily centralized political system is in place, one that decides when, how, and how much you can eat, establishing even the extent of your needs. Private property, on the other hand, guarantees individual freedom.

After the pandemic, this issue came to a head in a world so blatantly riven and unjust. It might be useful to make the super rich pay super taxes. It would be a good way to recover equilibrium. The rich effectively ought to pay more. Elon Musk, to cite an example, could be one of those people to tax at adequate rates. I followed the recent debates at Davos as well, and I found it interesting that there are billions of people open to discussing common objectives. Then I wondered: When these people return to their own countries, what will they do? What kind of legislation will they promote? Will they be laws in favor of the elite, the super rich, or will they meet the needs of the great masses of poor, spreading like wildfire? And when we talk about the poor, we do well to clarify that we are not talking about those in Africa who earn less than a dollar a day, but the middle and lower middle classes who risk falling into a condition of extreme fragility from which they can recover only with great difficulty. Better to speak of social justice based on the gospel, after which private property remains a fixed point to reformulate.

Are you effectively theorizing a property tax for the super rich?

I would say that this is one of the next challenges the Church will have to take a stance on. It will have to be discussed in light of the Church's social doctrine. Make those who have super wealth pay super taxes. Who were the millionaires who made excessive profits during the global emergency? Naturally, it's the gospel that presents the principles of social doctrine to be applied to daily situations as they develop.

Leo XIII laid the foundations of social doctrine with *Rerum Novarum*, but in his day, Amazon certainly did not exist. Today, one speaks of the Fourth Industrial Revolution, of the coming of digitalization and globalization. This will certainly be the subject of analysis and reflection for the next pontiff, applying Christology and salvation to modern life. There are frontiers that will require urgent responses from the Church; for example, whether microchips can be implanted under the skin to control a person's data or to make payments. And what the impact of the metaverse might be on people's lives. Clearly, the ability to control the masses is a temptation that moves against human dignity. I prefer to be observed by the eyes of God than by a Big Brother manipulator, with vested interests, whose boundaries often lack definition and whose true aims cannot be grasped. Where is the morality of the moralizers? Control is a seduction that has always existed, even in ancient Rome, when there were emperors who incarnated the ideals of power and fame and held in their hands the cult of false gods adored by the masses. A bit like today, with numerous VIP personalities of the Bill Gates type.

Does the Church consider globalization a threat or an opportunity?

It is only a factual reality that has to be dealt with. It is something that exists and moves and can bring positive effects. At this moment, given the evolution of matters, it presents shady areas. I'm referring to the spread of the digitalization of data, including personal data. This runs the risk of leading to widespread generalized control over people, as in China, where respect for the human person does not exist. The Catholic Church — the prime global player in the whole world — has the historical primacy in the principle of universality and respects the various cultures; it protects their development, and within her there is no unified culture.

The Second Vatican Council established precise limits of action. To understand better, take the image of Pentecost, with the Spirit who descended on everyone, not to unify or massify in one regional culture but rather to give space to each, with each one's own personality, history, and language, in the unity of the faith and Christ. It's a large family of cultures that believe in one God, the Savior of the world.

Let's return to the concept of private property.

The Church, I repeat, approves of private property. Within limits, it guarantees human dignity because it protects from the arbitrariness of the absolute state. Each person has the right to possess the means to sustain his life and his freedom. Private property is a basic principle and falls under the principles of the *bonum commune*. Translated into daily economic life, this means that entrepreneurs should be recognized for the strength of their entrepreneurial ideas; they have the duty to pay taxes and just wages. The state, according to the principle of the *bonum commune*, will ensure the construction of roads, universities, bridges. It goes without saying that when private property obstructs the common good, it has reached a limit.

What would you choose between Marxism and neo-capitalism?

I consider neo-Marxism to be more dangerous because it ends up with greater widespread power, in that it develops better when adapted to national situations. Nevertheless, unbridled liberalism and pure capitalism are harmful because they do not respect the human person but seek only profit. Consider the United States, where this form of neo-capitalism predominates, or even in China, where a link between capitalism and neo-Marxism of an atheist brand has spread. For this reason, it is wrong to speak of socialism in China because, as such, it does not exist.

Ideologies are not all the same, perhaps. Is there some aspect worth saving in Marx's Das Kapital, *in your opinion? For example, the fact of having been realized as a response to an economic model of exploitation and to bring out of poverty entire fragile sectors of society. Is not the path China has trodden that of having brought out of poverty hundreds of millions of people? According to the estimates of the World Bank, 850 million people have been emancipated — nearly a hundred million of them in the last ten years.*

Marx wanted to react to the Industrial Revolution and to all the consequences emerging in society, such as class differences. All the other forms of Marxism that developed later and that were based on atheistic materialism shared the same idea: that man is not a proper subject, not an independent person, but is subordinated to a superior reality that decides for him. If we consider the program undertaken by Lenin or Stalin, considering the tens of millions of victims left in their wake, perhaps certain positive rhetoric still attributed to their works would fall apart. Liberating millions of people from impoverished conditions is possible by other means.

Think of Germany after the war. It was divided in two: the eastern part, subjected to a Marxist economy, and the western part, where an open, democratic society was constructed. In West Germany, Konrad Adenauer, with all his limits, promoted a program inspired by the social doctrine of the Church, based on respect for the person.

Widening our gaze toward China, on the other hand, during Mao's regency, we cannot forget that sixty million people lost their lives and hundreds of millions were humiliated. Still today, there is no respect for the people. Just read the news and see how they are reacting to the Covid epidemic. The suicide rate is sky-high, not due to a lack of cures and medicine but out of desperation. The one-party, communist system blocks the idea of a free society respectful of human rights. The Church's social doctrine, on the other hand, surpasses both the socialist horizon as well as the capitalist one.

Take, for example, the encyclical *Centesimus Annus* of John Paul II. The concept of the free market is developed alongside that of solidarity and respect for man understood as a political social subject upon which biblical anthropology is based as well. God did not create man isolated from others. He infused the breath of life into a man and a woman in a harmonious vision projected toward future generations. In short: it's important to reconcile the concept of man understood as a person and the concept of man as a social element. In this framework, the state is excluded from the Church if it attempts to assume a function of absolute authority.

Can capitalism, then, be considered an absolute evil?

When money becomes the highest value of reference, a sort of absolute god, then something must be reconsidered. As an instrument, money is per se neutral; it depends on the use one makes of it. Thus, capitalism, as such, is not evil, but if capital remains concentrated in the hands of very few, the harmful effects for the community are multiplied, and harmonious development is hindered. This means there is a minority that is exploiting the majority. Naturally, this does not mean excluding the entrepreneurial category, the capable ones, people with organizational and ethical abilities. These are the people who, in the future, will have to cultivate vast projects, anchored in ethical principles, because the growth of some depends on the development of others.

There are great businessmen who act consciously according to social justice, who are concerned about their individual employees, considering them part of the broader family. Others, on the other hand, continue to aim at maximum profits and exploitation. The worst evil, according to the Bible, is avarice, which is at the origin of many defects.[31] Money per se is not to blame; it is only an instrument. It is

---

[31] See 1 Tim. 6:10: "The love of money is the root of all evils."

man who, more or less consciously, makes use of it in a distorted way to the point of becoming a sinner. "It is easier for a camel to go through the eye of a needle than for a rich man to enter the kingdom of God" (Matt. 19:24). Wine is not to blame if people get drunk and do damage. Great wealth can serve to corrupt or to carry out great works: it depends on what one has in his heart.

In his encyclical *Rerum Novarum*, Leo XIII faced the age-old social question of how to protect the common man and not the super rich, comparing two systems, nascent capitalism and communism. The Church seeks to develop private property in the hands of workers; she seeks to defend not so much the nabobs but the most fragile, the little owners who possess a home, a small bank account, life savings — the resources, that is, for realizing their freedom and independence.

Let's return to the Church's social doctrine.

It was not born with Leo XIII but has ancient roots, seeing that it originates from Christian anthropology, finding applications in new contexts. Before *Rerum Novarum*, there were important thinkers who left writings and reflections in this direction. A German bishop named Emmanuel von Ketteler of Mainz comes to mind. We German Catholics are very proud of him. He opposed Bismarck and defended the liberty of the Church. Above all, he had no doubts about giving a negative judgment to the ideas of Marx, to the point of opposing his theses. His was a Church that certainly did not support the powerful but, rather, the poor. This made Ketteler — although little known — one of the most influential bishops of the nineteenth century. Thanks to him, the workers' movement called Opera Kolping came to life. This was a notable reality founded by a priest, Adolph Kolping, beatified in 1991.

The Chinese Dilemma

Does the agreement that the pope signed and renewed with China re-
garding the nomination of bishops and the normalization of relations
between the two Chinese churches — the underground one, faithful to
Rome and therefore persecuted, and the patriotic one controlled by
the Communist Party — constitute a positive step toward obtaining
ultimately common ground between the Holy See and Beijing?

One mustn't make a deal with the devil. There are unknown clauses in
that agreement. For Chinese Catholic priests faithful to Rome, there are
formation courses planned in an obvious attempt to control Catholic
structures. There is a letter sent by Secretary of State Cardinal Pietro
Parolin in which Chinese priests are authorized to sign a document
that imposes these courses of indoctrination. Unfortunately, what
is happening in silence shows critical aspects that are very serious.
Most disconcerting is the culpable silence with which the Holy See
is facing this critical situation. Vatican diplomacy insists on saying we
need to be discreet, but if this continues, we will end up like Hilarion,
the Russian metropolitan transferred by Putin because he dared to
criticize the war in Ukraine.

The Chinese Catholic Church must not become a sort of state altar
boy, guaranteeing critical support to the Communist Party. It must

not serve the motives of the state. Ambrose, as bishop of Milan, did not hesitate to contest Emperor Theodosius. He was the last emperor of the united Roman Empire, responsible for a terrible massacre in Thessalonica that caused seven thousand deaths. When Theodosius wanted to enter the cathedral, Ambrose stopped him, demanding an act of penance, making it known that he would be treated like every other baptized Christian and that he should respect the principles of life and not kill the innocent. These are the great episcopal role models for the Church who should continue to inspire us.

In China, there is a man who has spent himself trying to oppose this problematic union, as well as the Beijing government. Cardinal Zen Ze-kiun, octogenarian former archbishop of Hong Kong, was arrested in May 2022 on accusations of conspiracy against the Chinese government favoring external powers.

Do you know him personally?

Who doesn't know him? I think he is completely in the right on this issue. In my opinion, he is a martyr of freedom, of Christian thinking, and of human dignity. He was even arrested and then released on bail, and the simple fact that he was detained offers a cross section of the environment he moves in.

This is not the first time a Communist regime has struck out at a prominent cardinal. It already happened in the past to giants such as the Croatian cardinal Stepinac in former Yugoslavia at the time of Tito; the Ukrainian cardinal Slipyj, arrested by the Soviet authorities; the Hungarian cardinal Mindszenty; and the Polish cardinal Wyszyński. In the case of Zen, the Holy See has never taken a clear position publicly. Until now, the Vatican has adopted a prudent attitude of caution, perhaps even ambivalence, avoiding making the situation worse, not risking negative chain reactions against Chinese Catholics.

And yet the Church ought to be a beacon for the defense of human rights according to a Christian vision, an evangelical witness. It ought to speak openly even in situations that concern states with regimes of a communist sort, in which civil liberties are limited, starting with religious liberty.

Why do you consider China to be a danger for the Church and for the world?

We can start immediately by clarifying that it is the China of Xi and not the Chinese people, as such, that is the potential threat because it tends to destroy freedom of conscience. Every man and woman must have the choice to seek the truth and decide freely, but in China, this does not happen. The danger lies in the ideology of those governing, of the governing class, and not the Chinese created by God, who merit the benefits of the grace of the gospel. The party has control over these people and presents itself with the dynamics of an absolute preexistent authority.

President Xi behaves almost like a god, becoming more absolute over the years, refusing to accept liberty of conscience, pluralism, and freedom of religion. He seeks to align, control, and level, to the point at which, today in China, believing in another god (other than Xi) is considered a crime, a hostile act. Crucifixes have been prohibited in the houses of Christians as well as crosses in many places in China. Add to this the fact that the party has learned to use mass means of communication, no less than platforms such as TikTok, to manipulate the Chinese with incessant propaganda. Whoever resists, such as the Muslim minority the Uyghurs, is punished with imprisonment and re-education camps. We are aware of only a small part of this reality and only because there have been news leaks. Thus, it became known that the Uyghurs were subjected to mistreatment and torture. Naturally, the Chinese denied it, but it is evident that the dictatorship is quite brutal.

China is politically and economically very strong and influential internationally, thanks also to the policy of penetration they are carrying out in Africa and in poor countries (naturally rich in raw materials). Even in Italy and in Greece, they are active in grabbing ports and strategic infrastructure. The Second Vatican Council is a beacon, carving out fundamental points on religious freedom, dignity, and freedom of conscience, which cannot be limited, not even by the state. It is our task as Christians to defend it.

Why are you so attentive to China?

How can one be unaware of this reality, in a world in ferment, where China is the most powerful state, with the biggest economy, and the most populous nation in the world? Human rights must be questioned first. The widespread blindness is worrisome. When Christianity was just beginning to spread and Rome was the head of an absolute state with the cult of the emperor, there existed an attitude much more permissive toward Christianity in the empire than in Beijing today. China under Xi, however, will not get the better of Christianity; it will not succeed in suffocating it. So we have to look forward, hoping to avoid persecution.

The Vatican signed an agreement with Beijing that normalized episcopal nominations. Don't you think that ultimately this is a valid accord?

Unfortunately, we do not know the contents of this agreement with the Vatican. They kept it secret. We should certainly consider the fundamental intention of this diplomatic step positively. It places as its objective the finding of a *modus vivendi* with the regime, similar to what took place in Germany with the concordat signed between the Church and Hitler. In that period during the pontificate of Pius XI, it was Cardinal Eugenio Pacelli, as secretary of state, and the German vice-chancellor Franz von Papen who signed it. The Vatican sought a compromise to contain the dangers.

The same thing can be said today as well with Communist China. The Vatican identified a route considered the lesser evil, in an attempt to reach an acceptable compromise. What makes me skeptical is that everyone who knows the Chinese situation well — Cardinal Zen, for example (though not the only one) — continues to repeat that the agreement is to the exclusive advantage of atheistic communism. The government has always been convinced that the Chinese Church should be directly responsible to another state, the Vatican, forgetting that the Church is a communion of the faithful. Given that I have never read the agreement, I cannot say if it should be considered a complete mistake or not. Nevertheless, it is interesting to note that when they signed in Beijing, the Vatican delegation consisted of relatively few Catholic representatives (obviously, Cardinal Pietro Parolin, the secretary of state was among them). Chinese theologians were not present in the commission. When Pius XI promulgated the encyclical *Mit Brennender Sorge*, he carried out long consultations with the German bishops. The Chinese accord, to the contrary, lacks the opinions of local experts.

One must ask whether this agreement might be useful in the future, but first one needs to respond to another question: Which future? In the end, I see only a Church that risks being compliant, subservient to party politicians. It's possible that an ideal vision of China was transmitted to the pope, a mythical model of a distant epic in which the Jesuits of Matteo Ricci's age had a big role.

Recently, I had occasion to listen to a bishop who assured me that in China the civil authorities are carrying out the Church's social doctrine because they have eradicated poverty for hundreds of millions of people. Naturally, my eyes popped out. I couldn't believe what I was hearing: everyone knows that Beijing does not respect the essence of the person, freedom, individual faith. This issue cannot be relativized in this way because it undermines human coexistence. Another theme the Church will have to resume in her public preaching in the future is so-called gender ideology, whose effects are so pernicious.

Are you concerned about the Taiwan issue and the clash between the United States and China, since Beijing considers it a rebellious island and intends to proceed with "reunification" and normalization, as happened in Hong Kong?

The case of Taiwan is quite serious and emblematic. The people of Taiwan should be supported in their right to self-determination. They are a people living in a democratic system and have expressed their desire not to become part of China and be absorbed by the one government in Beijing — exactly like the Ukrainians, who do not want to become part of Russia. As Christians, we are asked to defend the principles of truth and justice in every part of the world.

To put it more concretely, recently the Vatican has floated the possibility of reducing the diplomatic level of the embassy of the Holy See situated in Taiwan. This would be a deleterious signal. If this happened, it would be like a concession to extortion on the part of Beijing. And we must not allow ourselves to be blackmailed. Therefore, it is better to continue working toward acceptable compromises, as long as these do not have a bearing on the terrain of human rights and on the will of Taiwan to decide autonomously where to go and how to live in the future. If the opposite happens, the Holy See risks becoming a partner in a terrible power struggle. St. Paul, in his letter to Timothy, says that the pillar of truth will triumph (see 1 Tim. 3:15). Every nation has material, political, and economic interests to defend. I hope the Church has the lucidity to hold fast to her position *super partes*, without selfish interests, based solely on the light of the Word of God.

The Holy See has been silent on Hong Kong during these years of slippage into repression and has never said a thing about the "Umbrella Revolution" or against the liberticidal laws that have been passed by the former British colony.

Unfortunately, that silence weighs heavily. It was unjust to stay silent. It was a very grave error, in my opinion, attributable to the logic of Vatican diplomacy, forgetful that we Catholics, if we do not raise our voice to defend these abnormal cases, we are not even defending Christian principles. The fear that hides behind this omitted condemnation lies in the fact that the Chinese government blackmailed the Vatican. The government made it known that it could vindicate itself on the Catholic residents in Hong Kong or in China. Once again, history teaches us not to commit the same errors.

The silence of the Vatican in the face of Hitler's blackmail, when, to avoid persecution, they omitted clear denunciation of what was happening in all of Germany. The gospel asks us to shout the truth from the rooftops, to work for the weak and the persecuted. Even Jesus told Pilate he came to give witness to the truth. Undeniably, we cannot provoke the powerful; if anything, our task is to teach how to distinguish the true from the false, the good from the bad. Did Francis not strongly condemn the mafia of Piana di Gioia Tauro,[32] excommunicating them? Clearly, the communists in the Beijing government cannot be excommunicated as some were by Pius XII (also because they are not Catholics). Nevertheless, it would be preferable if they found the courage to proffer a few words in support of the truth.

---

[32] In June 2014.

Just a diplomatic error?

An enormous blunder. We can trace it back to a defect dating from Paul VI's reform of the Roman Curia. In the agreement signed with Beijing, they decided to assign to the papacy and to Rome the primacy in diplomacy. Implicitly, it was established that first comes diplomacy and only after, dogma and truth. But the Church founded by Jesus Christ is not the Church that has the Vatican City as its state. Over time, two dimensions were comingled, though they were not meant to be confused. The same setup is reflected in the text signed in Beijing. It comes to mind how the role assumed by President Xi is starting to approach veneration due to God. Every child and even adults, including Catholics, have to study his book, or the bible of Mao, as if they were the words of a mythological divinity. The Church must fight for true democracy and for the protection of human rights without abdicating the task of speaking openly and fearlessly about the gospel. Even in the face of conflicts, controversies, and debates.

And yet the Vatican's diplomatic school has a long cursus honorum and many glorious chapters.

It's obvious that the Holy See's diplomacy conducts many useful negotiations around the world and succeeds in mediating peace between warring groups, advocates for petitions, facilitates processes of peace-keeping. Nevertheless, it cannot prevail over primary dimensions, to the point of reaching political agreements like the one with China, while neglecting truth and justice. The Church cannot make compromises with illiberal political regimes.

What happened in the Philippines comes to mind, where a president ordered the murder of many fragile people to resolve their drug problem. In the face of this slaughter, the Church did not raise a strong, clear protest. What I mean to say is that, in the future, we need to live our exemplary prophetic vocation on this ever more asymmetric, international chessboard, a vocation not dependent on the scales of diplomacy. The Church has divine foundations. We are servants of God who must fight, speak, and defend the poor and the persecuted. The truth will make us free, we repeat as we read the Gospel (John 8:32). We must not think only of what politicians do or would do, because that cannot be our measuring rod. Jesus never entered Herod's palace.

But in certain situations, how can the Church not engage in politics?

I didn't say that, and that's not how it is. If the Church must mix, enter, and become a leaven in order to present to the political world the moral horizon, she mustn't seek power or compromise that can amputate Christian principles. The Vatican is not a state that wants to expand its sphere of influence, to dominate or invade. The Church has the vocation of uniting diverse peoples, not engaging in politics on behalf of a state. And the pope's authority cannot be applied in siding with or endorsing a particular politician, affirming more or less discreetly, "I'm for him and not for her!" The Church has the duty to speak clearly every time she recognizes the need — above all, when the political sphere does not carry out its duty, when it fails to organize programs for the common good of its citizens, when it undermines peace abroad, when it fails to respect social justice, when it does not guarantee the necessary infrastructure, and when it weakens the architecture on which human society is based. The Church must speak with the enduring voice of the gospel.

About the Authors

Gerhard Ludwig Müller (b. 1947) is the archbishop emeritus of Regensburg, Germany. The second German after Joseph Ratzinger to lead the Congregation for the Doctrine of the Faith, he has a profound knowledge of modern theology and has dedicated his life to the study of Christian comprehension of revelation, ecclesiology, and ecumenism.

Franca Giansoldati is a journalist and Vatican correspondent with the Italian daily *Messaggero*. Among her books are *Il demonio in Vaticano. I Legionari di Cristo e il caso Maciel* [The demon in the Vatican: The Legionaries of Christ and the Maciel case] (2014), *La marcia senza ritorno* [The march of no return] (2015), *L'alfabeto verde di Papa Francesco* [The green alphabet of Pope Francis] (2019), and, with Lucetta Scaraffia and Anna Foa, *Agnus Dei. Gli abusi sessuali del clero in Italia* [Agnus Dei: sexual abuse in the Italian clergy] (2022).

Sophia Institute

Sophia Institute is a nonprofit institution that seeks to nurture the spiritual, moral, and cultural life of souls and to spread the gospel of Christ in conformity with the authentic teachings of the Roman Catholic Church.

Sophia Institute Press fulfills this mission by offering translations, reprints, and new publications that afford readers a rich source of the enduring wisdom of mankind.

Sophia Institute also operates the popular online resource CatholicExchange.com. *Catholic Exchange* provides world news from a Catholic perspective as well as daily devotionals and articles that will help readers to grow in holiness and live a life consistent with the teachings of the Church.

In 2013, Sophia Institute launched Sophia Institute for Teachers to renew and rebuild Catholic culture through service to Catholic education. With the goal of nurturing the spiritual, moral, and cultural life of souls, and an abiding respect for the role and work of teachers, we strive to provide materials and programs that are at once enlightening to the mind and ennobling to the heart; faithful and complete, as well as useful and practical.

Sophia Institute gratefully recognizes the Solidarity Association for preserving and encouraging the growth of our apostolate over the course of many years. Without their generous and timely support, this book would not be in your hands.

www.SophiaInstitute.com
www.CatholicExchange.com
www.SophiaInstituteforTeachers.org

Sophia Institute Press is a registered trademark of Sophia Institute.
Sophia Institute is a tax-exempt institution as defined by the
Internal Revenue Code, Section 501(c)(3). Tax ID 22-2548708.